Teachers' Professional Ethics

Moral Development and Citizenship Education

VOLUME 20

The titles published in this series are listed at *brill.com/mora*

Teachers' Professional Ethics

Theoretical Frameworks and Empirical Research from Finland

By

Kirsi Tirri and Elina Kuusisto

BRILL

LEIDEN | BOSTON

All chapters in this book have undergone peer review.

Library of Congress Cataloging-in-Publication Data

Names: Tirri, Kirsi, author. | Kuusisto, Elina, author.
Title: Teachers' professional ethics : theoretical frameworks and empirical
  research from Finland / by Kirsi Tirri and Elina Kuusisto.
Description: Leiden ; Boston : Brill, 2022. | Series: Moral development and
  citizenship education, 2352-5770 ; volume 20 | Includes bibliographical
  references and index.
Identifiers: LCCN 2022038796 (print) | LCCN 2022038797 (ebook) | ISBN
  9789004532625 (paperback) | ISBN 9789004532632 (hardback) | ISBN
  9789004532649 (ebook)
Subjects: LCSH: Teachers--Professional ethics--Finland. | Education--Moral
  and ethical aspects--Finland.
Classification: LCC LB1779 .T57 2022 (print) | LCC LB1779 (ebook) | DDC
  371.10094897--dc23/eng/20220818
LC record available at https://lccn.loc.gov/2022038796
LC ebook record available at https://lccn.loc.gov/2022038797

Typeface for the Latin, Greek, and Cyrillic scripts: "Brill". See and download: brill.com/brill-typeface.

ISSN 2352-5770
ISBN 978-90-04-53262-5 (paperback)
ISBN 978-90-04-53263-2 (hardback)
ISBN 978-90-04-53264-9 (e-book)

Contents

Preface

We have written this research-based book on teachers' professional ethics to increase understanding of the moral nature of the teaching profession. The book is intended for international readers who want to learn the theoretical frameworks that guide teachers' ethics and that help them address concrete challenges in their everyday work. Many international scholars have identified Finland as an exemplar country in education and teacher education. However, in recent years, our country has faced increasing challenges in education, mostly in issues related to equality and equity. These issues have impacted teachers' ethical thinking and conduct, and we have taken them into account in our discussion. Scholars and teachers from different countries can use this book to widen their understanding of teacher ethics and the Finnish educational system.

Finnish education is research-based, which means that in Finland university teachers research what they teach and teach what they research. Kirsi Tirri is a Professor of Education at the University of Helsinki, and she teaches a basic course in school pedagogy each year to 800 pre-service teachers training to work in fields ranging from early education to adult education. She also leads the School Pedagogy Research Group, which includes docents, post-doctoral researchers, and doctoral and master's students.

Docent Elina Kuusisto has been Kirsi Tirri's master's and doctoral student and is now a senior member of the School Pedagogy Research Group. She is also a lecturer at Tampere University. In this book, we present our group's main research findings related to teachers' work and ethics. As early as 1996–1999, the Academy of Finland funded Kirsi Tirri's research on moral dilemmas in schools, and this project produced important publications that have been cited widely and are also referenced in this book. We built another project, Teachers' Moral Competence in Pedagogical Encounters (MoCo) based on these research findings and developed a Finnish teaching module for the European Union Erasmus project Education for Democratic Intercultural Citizenship (EDIC+), funded for the years 2016–2019. This module is offered every second year to international students in the University of Helsinki's master's programme Changing Education. In this module, our teaching concentrates on three important factors that affect teachers' moral behavior: teachers' ethical sensitivity, purposeful teaching, and teachers' implicit beliefs (mindsets) (Kuusisto & Tirri, 2019).

Kirsi Tirri was a visiting scholar at the Center on Adolescence at Stanford University, directed by Professor William Damon, between 2007 and 2016.

During this period, we adapted his concept of purpose to our studies on teachers and students. We also participated in the project How Service-learning Influences Youth Purpose around the World, led by Research Associate Professor Seana Moran and funded by the John Templeton foundation for the years 2014–2017. As a result, the article-based doctoral dissertations of two of our students, Niina Manninen (2019) and Nasibeh Hedayati (2019), included articles that addressed the purposes of social service workers and Iranian secondary school students. We also developed the concept of purposeful teaching (Tirri, Moran, & Mariano, 2016) and the purposeful teacher (Tirri, 2018) as goals of teacher education and ethical teaching.

Kirsi Tirri was a research director at the Helsinki Collegium for Advanced Studies during the years 2017–2019. During that time, she designed the Copernicus-project Changing Mindsets about Learning: Connecting Psychological, Educational, and Neuroscientific Evidence. Professor Carol Dweck, from Stanford University, is the Academic Advisor of this project, and we have applied her mindset theory to our multidisciplinary studies on teaching and learning. Junfeng Zhang (2020) compared the mindsets of Chinese and Finnish students and teachers in her doctoral dissertation, and Cristiana Levinthal (2022) has explored the mindsets of Portuguese and Finnish parents related to their children's learning. Teachers' implicit beliefs (mindsets) influence their ethics and teaching behavior, and it is important to reveal and change those beliefs that are unethical or discriminate against students.

In this book we discuss teachers' professional ethics using both theoretical and empirical approaches. We provide examples of concrete moral dilemmas in teaching that can be more effectively navigated with the rational principles and guidelines that philosophies of different ethical frameworks can provide. We argue that teachers require ethical skills, especially *ethical sensitivity*, in order to select the most beneficial course of action concerning diverse students in inclusive education. Moreover, they should be *purposeful* in their profession to develop the motivation and resilience to continue their demanding but fulfilling work with long-term goals. Moreover, they should acknowledge their *implicit beliefs and possible stereotypes* to be able to provide equal learning opportunities to their students and to build democratic moral communities in their schools. In this book, ethical sensitivity, purposeful teaching, and incremental beliefs concerning learning are seen as important prerequisites for teachers' professional ethics. We discuss these aspects with examples from our empirical studies in Finnish schools.

The book can also be used in different countries as a self-study teacher-education course book. For this purpose, we have added questions for readers to reflect upon after each chapter to help them process the different concepts and research findings presented in the book. To provide comparative perspectives on the topics discussed, we compare the case of Finnish education with examples from different countries.

We would like to thank our previous publishers, especially the *Journal of Moral Education*, for publishing our articles from 1999 until the present day (Tirri, 1999b; Husu & Tirri, 2001; Malin, Tirri, & Liauw, 2015; Hedayati, Kuusisto, Gholami, & Tirri, 2017c; Manninen, Kuusisto, & Tirri, 2018; Rissanen, Kuusisto, Hanhimäki, & Tirri, 2018; Ronkainen, Kuusisto, Eisenschmidt, & Tirri, 2021). Moreover, we would like to thank the Brill book series *Moral Development and Citizenship Education* and the series editors Fritz Oser and Wiel Veugelers for publishing our books (Tirri, 2008; Tirri & Nokelainen, 2011; Kuusisto, Ubani, Nokelainen, & Toom, 2021). In addition, Gaudeamus Helsinki University Press has published our book on teachers' ethics in Finnish (Tirri & Kuusisto, 2019), and we would like to thank the Publishing Director, Leena Kaakinen, for her valuable collaboration. Feedback from Helsinki University Press has also helped us to improve the manuscript of this book. We are grateful for the anonymous three experts who provided valuable suggestions for improvement in their referee comments of our first draft of the manuscript. We would also like to thank Wiel Veugelers and John Bennett for their comments and support in the final modifications of the book.

We dedicate this book to Fritz Oser, the first editor of the series Moral Development and Citizenship Education. His research work on teachers' ethos and moral education has had an important influence on our thinking and teaching. We hope that this book can continue Fritz's legacy and honor him as a great scholar and wonderful human being.

Figures and Tables

Figures

Tables

CHAPTER 1

Introduction

Teachers in many countries are ethical professionals whose value base rests upon a national ethical code for teachers and the national core curricula. In this book we present these important ethical guidelines with Finnish examples and discuss other ethical frameworks that help teachers solve moral dilemmas they encounter in their work. Teachers require rational principles that they can use to find answers to the current challenges in education in Finland and abroad. Moreover, when different societal crises arise, teachers also require resilience and purpose to continue to work in the profession. According to UNESCO (2021), the world will soon face a substantial teacher shortage. We will need 69 million elementary and secondary school teachers by the year 2030. By then, it is likely that 258 million children will receive no formal education, and this number does not include those who dropped out because of the Covid-19 pandemic. Moreover, 800 million young people and adults lack basic skills in mathematics and literacy, without which they will be unable to find employment.

In Finland, we have been lucky to attract gifted young people to teaching, especially females, who have been able to realize their academic and artistic talents in their work as teachers (Tirri, 2014). However, the current global crises have influenced teacher education and teachers' work in Finland too, and thus it is important to promote crisis resilience in future teachers.

We face various kinds of crises, which can be 'predictable or unexpected, global or local, one-dimensional or multidimensional, fast or slow, or easy or difficult to handle' (Mauranen et al., 2021, p. 9). In a statement issued by the Finnish Academy of Science and Letters titled *Bending, but not breaking – From the coronavirus pandemic to strengthening Finland's crisis resilience*, a group of leading scholars discussed different ways to develop crisis management (Mauranen et al., 2021). Finland is known for its strong education system and high-levels of societal trust, which were key factors in the country's relative success in managing the pandemic. Thus, it is important to maintain these Finnish characteristics in the future. One way to achieve this is to promote equality and equal opportunities for education in society. Education is extremely important for providing a sense of safety and security within society and helps lay the foundation for a better future in the midst of various crises. Moreover, effective communication is required between different parties to negotiate different solutions to these crises. Interaction is also essential in a democratic society to promote inclusion and participation.

Formal education is key to supporting life-long learning and the experience of a meaningful life by providing equal opportunities for schooling. However, the Finnish population is becoming ever more diverse, with consequent implications for educational equality. The challenge is now to help those families with low educational and income status encourage their children to seek further education. In recent years, Finland has enhanced the opportunities for digital learning in education. However, the coronavirus pandemic revealed not only the strengths but also the weaknesses of distance learning. Finnish schools were fast to adjust to online teaching, but it was not suitable for all students and teachers (Mauranen et al., 2021).

It is not only global crises that influence teachers' work. Teachers encounter everyday challenges, conflicts, and dilemmas that are ethical in nature and also address issues of equality and inclusion. Professional ethics are required for every teacher to reflect on and solve these daily situations. The focus of this book is the teaching profession and the ethical core of teaching. The goal of education is to help students find their own agency and strengthen it at all grade levels and in all school subjects. The goal of the teaching profession is to help students grow, and this goal includes supporting the development of students' purpose, both in their studies and in life, with a view to the future. The book offers both research-based knowledge and concrete pedagogical ideas to support this goal.

The book is written from a school pedagogy and general didactics perspective. It is based on the German and Nordic didactical tradition, which aims to support individuals' holistic development to become civilized members of society (Kansanen et al., 2000). We also connect these concepts to Anglo-American theories based on educational psychology, which are investigated in the light of the empirical data we have gathered during the last 10 years.

Schools require teachers with a long-term commitment to teaching and a sense of the meaningfulness of their profession. To this end, educators need knowledge of the different ethical frameworks underpinning teacher ethics. In Chapter 2, we present these frameworks, thereby building the theoretical and philosophical foundation to investigate the ethical aspects of teachers' work. Prior to the end of the 20th century, ethics and morality in teaching had long been taken for granted and thus under-researched. However, in the 1990s, scholarly interest in teacher ethics and moral dilemmas in teaching dramatically increased (Jackson et al., 1993; Sockett, 1993; Tirri, 1999). This emphasis and the abundance of research on teachers' ethics in the 1990s explains why we refer to many publications and research findings from this era. These are considered to be seminal studies in the literature on teacher ethics (see, e.g., Osguthorpe, 2021).

In this book, we emphasize the ethics of commitment in teachers' work. Teacher commitment has long been reflected in Finnish educational policy. In 1998, an ethical code for teachers was published, and, in 2017, the trend continued with the establishment of Comenius' Oath. In the school community, a teacher is committed to students and colleagues and other possible collaborating partners. In this book, we view teachers as life-long learners who can and should develop throughout their entire career. In Chapter 3, we emphasize the development of ethical expertise, skills in distributing justice, ethical decision making, and readiness to engage in ethical discussions. We highlight the rational principles guiding teachers' thinking and actions by drawing on the cognitive moral tradition advocated by Lawrence Kohlberg in moral education and Fritz Oser in teacher education. To provide a comprehensive overview of the different schools of thought influencing the moral domain in education, we also present thoughts from those scholars who emphasize intuition, virtues, and caring in the development of ethical expertise in teaching.

Chapter 4 discusses the growing diversity in schools and the reasons why the whole learning community requires *ethical sensitivity* in identifying and solving ethical issues. Every teacher is a moral educator, and their teaching both includes moral messages and reflects their educational philosophy. In this chapter, moral dilemmas and conflicts are discussed from the perspective of teachers, students, parents, and principals to provide a holistic picture of the school as a moral community. We also present a self-report instrument developed to evaluate the ethical sensitivity skills of teachers and students and the empirical results from this instrument in different cultural contexts. The culture-specific and culture-invariant aspects of ethical sensitivity that we identified from these findings inform teachers' understanding of their students' diverse cultural backgrounds.

Our research adapts William Damon's (2008) holistic developmental theory of a purpose in life to teacher education and teachers' professional development. In Chapter 5, we present the concept of a *purposeful teacher*, which we use to describe teachers who can combine their personal purpose in life with their long-term commitment to teaching (Tirri, 2018; Kuusisto & Tirri, 2021). Purposeful teachers, in turn, help their students find a sustainable and long-term purpose in their studies and wider lives. This chapter presents a didactical model that allows teachers to elaborate the meaning of the subject they teach. Especially in times of crisis, purpose is required to provide teachers with the resilience necessary to continue their work and to help students remain motivated to study.

Teachers require ethically sustainable means to meet the needs of diverse learners and address pedagogical challenges in teaching. In Chapter 6, we argue that implicit beliefs guide teachers' actions, and thus teachers should acknowledge the impact of their beliefs on their professional ethics. To aid teachers in this task, we have developed a *growth mindset pedagogy* adapted from Carol Dweck's (2000, 2006) theory on the two different implicit beliefs, i.e., mindsets, that guide our thinking about teaching and learning. Implicit beliefs are important for teachers' professional ethics because they might include stereotypes that hinder the provision of equal learning opportunities to all students. Moreover, it is necessary for teachers to acknowledge those implicit beliefs held by their students that prevent them from learning and realizing their full potential in certain areas, such as mathematics.

We summarize and reiterate the main message of our book in Chapter 7, that the ideas and empirical findings we present can be used to improve teachers' pre- and in-service education. In order to build schools as democratic moral communities, we require teachers with knowledge of multiple ethical frameworks that can be used to rationally justify the principles behind their moral arguments and actions. Teachers need knowledge of the ethical principles guiding their work and the willingness to commit to their profession with long-term goals. We emphasize ethical sensitivity skills in that can be taught and learned like other elements of ethical expertise, including distributing justice, decision making, and ethical discussion. Building moral communities requires resilience from teachers. In this task, teachers need sustainable life purposes and the ability to guide their students to find meaningful goals for their life and studies. By recognizing and changing the implicit beliefs that hinder learning, teachers promote equal opportunities and the participation of diverse students in building schools as moral communities.

Teaching as an Ethical Profession

1 Development of Professional Ethics in Recent Decades

Teachers' work can be viewed in various ways in different countries. For instance, it can be seen as a job where the teacher fulfils certain standards and duties assigned by the authorities, as in the UK and the US (Harrison, 2019). In Finland, teaching is considered one of the professions. The discussion on teacher professionalism was prominent in Finland during the 1980s and 1990s, a theme that was also reflected in the academic literature and textbooks of the 1990s (Airaksinen, 1998; Tirri, 1999a). Traditionally, one criterion for the status of a profession has been academic education, in which intellectual skills are emphasized alongside the provision of services that promote essential wellbeing in society (Tirri, 1999a). Such professionals, in addition to teachers, include medical doctors, lawyers, psychologists and social workers. Occupations that meet the requirement of a profession possess systems of professional ethics, which play a major role in reflection on ethical challenges in the occupation, and ethical codes that help professionals meet these challenges (Tirri, 1999a). In the teaching profession, the most important factor in teachers' professional ethics is commitment to students and support for their learning and personal development.

Codes for teachers' professional conduct were published in the United States as early as the 1950s and 1970s, while in Europe they became more popular during the 1990s (Tirri, 1999a). Currently, more than 50 countries around the world have code of ethics for teachers (Forster, 2019). Such codes have been seen as an attempt to resolve the tension between autonomy and control in teachers' work. For example, Edward Terhart proposes that the compilation of teacher's ethical code in Germany was a compromise between idealizing the teacher's personality and the strict standardization of teaching. The emphasis on and idealization of teachers' personalities in professional ethics can cause the profession to be seen as a vocation in which only certain types of people can succeed. This kind of idealization can be viewed as a form of control, where teachers are made to feel guilty and inadequate if they fail to conform to this ideal. At the other end of the spectrum, teachers' work is controlled by standardization and defining professional duties in great detail. In this case, the evaluation of teachers' work becomes the primary means of controlling teachers (Terhart, 1998).

In Finland, teachers enjoy extensive freedom in their work, which in not controlled by any form of external evaluation. Finnish teachers are viewed as ethical professionals with the competence to reflect on their own work and develop in the profession with the help of pre-service and in-service education (Sahlberg, 2011; Tirri, 2014). In 1998, the Trade Union of Education in Finland published an ethical code for teachers, the first of its kind in the Nordic countries. The Finnish code is purposely formulated extremely loosely in order to be applicable to the work of all kinds of teachers (see the current code from 2010 in the Annex). Nevertheless, the code clearly demonstrates the current ideal of a 'general teacher' in which teachers of all subjects and grade-levels are seen as professional educators (Tirri, 2010). The following conclusions can be drawn from Finnish teachers' ethical code:

- The Finnish code openly express the values on which they are based.
- The code acknowledges teachers' own needs and rights in addition to the needs of students and society.
- The code acknowledges the communal nature of professional ethics by emphasizing interaction among teachers.
- The teaching profession is seen as part of Finnish society and teachers as playing an important role in building that society.

The Finnish ethical code for teachers is aspirational in nature rather than deontological (Schwimmer & Maxwell, 2017). The purpose of the code is not to provide concrete advice for ethical action but to remind teachers of the principles to which they are committed in their profession. It is the task and challenge of individual teachers to reflect on the application of these principles in the ethical questions they encounter. It specifies the underlying conception of humankind and the values derived from this conception: human dignity, truthfulness, justice, responsibility and freedom.

In an EU-project exploring common values in Europe, 12 EU-member states participated in an evaluation of how the values of democracy and tolerance are manifested in their official curricula for students in secondary education (Veugelers et al., 2017). The Finnish case study identified ethics and equality as important aspects of Finnish education policy (Tirri, 2017). According to participants in the Finnish study, the values propounded in official documents were not always actualized in schools. Moreover, teachers often lacked awareness of these values in their own national curriculum. In Finland, each municipality and school are required to establish local curricula and their own values to promote local perspectives; therefore, national and global factors are easily ignored. The Finnish ethical code for teachers emphasizes democracy and human dignity, and these values should be advanced by acknowledging global perspectives, including those of developing countries.

2   **Ethical Frameworks in Professional Ethics**

We argue that teachers' professional ethics are not governed by a single, all-encompassing ethical framework covering all aspects of their profession. Instead, professional ethics can be built on many different theories, each with its own goals and purposes. Some theories aim to acquire empirical knowledge and form predictions on that basis; others are interested in defining and clarifying the concepts used. For most of them, however, the unifying factor is that they are normative. The best-known theories in moral philosophy are strongly normative and take a clear stand on the values behind right thinking and action. Most of these theories provide some universal principle that can guide the teacher to reach the morally right decision. In teacher education, it is important to learn and reflect on these theories from the perspective of teachers' ethics. Below, we provide some examples of how teachers can justify their decisions based on these theories.

2.1   *Teleological and Deontological Ethics*
The term *teleological* comes from the Greek word *telos* and means the result or the final goal. Teleological theories are consequential ethical theories that emphasize the consequences of moral action. Thus, right action is determined by the result or consequence of the action.

According to teleological ethics, the consequences determine the kind of action that serves the best interest of the student. Therefore, if we adopt teleological ethics in education, we will pay most attention to educational goals. The most important task of the school is thus to promote the best interest of students according to the goals of education. Traditionally, schools have emphasized cognitive goals. According to teleological ethics, knowledge and its acquisition can be seen as the best interest of students and the goal teachers should attain in their work. A teacher's role is to function as the mediator of the most valid and correct knowledge. The goal of education is to find the truth.

A teleological ethical framework is relatively easy to utilize in the basic task of defining educational goals. This framework, however, fails to provide solutions to concrete dilemmas in the school community where the views of different groups are in conflict.

The best-known school of thought representing teleological ethics is utilitarianism. According to classic *utilitarianism*, we should always act in ways that provide the greatest amount of happiness to the largest number of people (Driver, 2014). By adopting this principle, the school community should function in a manner that profits the majority of its students. In school communities where the interests of different groups are in conflict, the application of utilitarian ethics should further the interests of the greatest number of students. However, this ethical framework can, in extreme cases, ignore objective truth in the advancement of the interests of the majority. In the worst cases, it can lead to a form of subjectivism which indorses majority values that directly conflict with the ideals of a democratic society. It is also extremely important to acknowledge the societal sphere beyond the school community and emphasize the wellbeing of future members of our society.

In contrast to teleological frameworks, deontological ethics emphasizes duties (Alexander & Moore, 2020). The term *deontological* comes from the Greek word *deon*, which means a duty or 'the one that binds.' According to the best-known advocate of deontological ethics, Immanuel Kant (1724–1804), the consequences of an act are irrelevant when evaluating its moral quality. This means, for example, that stealing is always wrong, regardless of the consequences. Thus, even if stealing could save somebody's life, it is not justified based on a strict Kantian doctrine.

Kantian ethics apply the categorial imperative in justifying right action (Rohlf, 2020). According to this approach, teachers should always act according to generally justifiable principles that define our universal duties to each other. The categorial imperative means, for example, that teachers' duties include respect for their students. However, deontological duty ethics lead, in practice, to a situation in which teachers cannot compromise on these principles, regardless of the consequences. Moreover, a duty such as respect for students requires sensitivity from a teacher, when, for example, protecting students' physical integrity.

Nevertheless, some advocates of deontological ethics interpret duty ethics less strictly. W.D. Ross (1877–1971) identified the main duties that can conflict with one another. These include the universal duty to avoid causing harm, to compensate for the damage we have inflicted, to do good, to be loyal, to be honest and grateful, to develop ourselves and to be just. According to Ross, in situations where these duties are in conflict, we should identify those duties that are most important to fulfil. While he provides no precise guidance on how to prioritize such duties, he claims that avoiding causing harm and keeping promises are more important than doing good. Moreover, Ross argues that in moral judgment we also require intuition and knowledge of the situation to complement rational thinking (Ross, 1930; Lebacqz, 1985).

Some schools of thought in ethics have adopted aspects from both teleological and deontological frameworks, thereby raising new and important issues for ethical reflection. For example, advocates of *critical theory*, such as Paolo Freire (1921–1997), wish to pay special attention to certain groups or minorities, due to their weaker societal status. These scholars frequently criticize current practices in the school community and seek to protect the rights of particular student groups, such as immigrants or female students. Moreover, advocates of this group might defend the rights of all students in the school community vis-à-vis those of teachers and administrators. For example, critical theorists have condemned the current school system for making students passive and voiceless. Freire's views on social justice, empowerment and transformation have important implications for moral education and teachers' professional ethics in emphasizing societal awareness and inclusion (Veugelers, 2017).

2.2   *Virtue Ethics*

Virtue ethics theories can be considered a branch of teleological ethics. Their goal is to promote the happy life of the individual as a member of a just community (Hursthouse & Pettigrove, 2018). The majority of normative moral theories are predominantly interested in guiding correct moral reasoning and action. Even though some of these theories acknowledge the influence of intuitive thinking and situational factors on moral reasoning, the main emphasis is rational thinking. However, in teachers' work it is difficult to separate professional and rational thinking from the teacher's own personality (Tirri et al., 1999). Teachers work and reflect on ethical problems in the light of their own values, beliefs and feelings. Thus, professional ethics cannot be reduced to a collection of ethical principles and the moral theories underlying them. This is why teachers should acknowledge their own ethical ideals and the individuals and groups whose values have most strongly influenced the development of their own ethical thinking. When teachers are faced with difficult ethical questions, they should ask themselves: 'What kind of person would I like to be?'; 'What kind of ethical decisions would the person I would like be to make?', and 'Is the decision I am making in harmony with my own personality and the ideals I am striving for in my life?'

Aristotle (384–322 BCE) was an example of a moral philosopher who advocated virtue ethics but did not separate individuals' personal qualities from their rational thinking. He used the term phronesis to refer to moral knowledge, which he considered intuitive and situational. According to Aristotelian knowledge, a person's prior attitudes and character traits influence what they perceive as ethically problematic and how they solve these problems (Aristotle, 1975; Bricker, 1993; Tirri & Husu, 2002). Ethical reasoning that is based on normative theories emphasizes rationality and the use of certain situation-dependent principles. However, teachers' personalities affect what they perceive as important in situations that call for moral reasoning. For example, a teacher who believes in positive thinking and finding the good in every child is likely to discern more positive issues than a teacher who looks for mistakes and thinks in a more negative manner. Thus, a student who constantly comments and interrupts the teacher can be seen as either a problematic individual who disturbs the lesson or as an energetic person interested in the learning task.

In the Aristotelian framework, the challenge in ethical problem-solving is to develop the sensitivity to identify the most important aspect of the situation. Application of the principles of moral theories will not help the teacher distinguish the issues that are important in each situation. For example, a student quarrel can equally be a playful incident between friends or the start of a serious conflict that requires immediate attention from the teacher (Tirri, 1999b). Usually, the interpretation of this kind of situation requires, in addition to rational thinking from the teacher, experience, intuition and skills in anticipating what will occur next. Consequently, for the development of professional ethics, it is important for teachers to learn ethical sensitivity in addition to moral reasoning and practice in order to distinguish the most salient moral factors from less important ones.

Many experts in professional ethics encourage trust in intuition as an addition to rational thinking (Nash, 2002; Dreyfus & Dreyfus, 1990). This means that teachers can utilize their feelings to help them solve ethical problems. Feelings are often necessary for the development of empathy and understanding. Teachers can engage their ethical sensitivity by asking which solution is best in harmony with their highest moral ideals, whether their actions run contrary to their personality, and whether the same solution would have been reached by their 'moral exemplar.'

Moral exemplars influence our ideas of the kinds of virtues a teacher should possess. Many exemplars are historical figures, such as Socrates and Jesus, who were renowned teachers. It is beneficial for teachers to recognize the moral exemplars who might have affected their thinking, even unconsciously. Moral exemplars are committed to high ideals, act according to them and take risks to uphold them. They are inspiring, humble and committed to their duties. They also identify with the needs of other people (Damon & Colby, 2015).

According to the Aristotle's teaching, moral virtues develop from habits and are best learned in homes and nearby environments. Virtues are necessary components of a happy life. From the perspective of virtue ethics, teachers' ethical solutions derive from their personality and virtues. A good and just teacher reaches good and just solutions. Virtue ethics focus on personal characteristics and the possibility to develop one's character through education (Harrison, 2019). Virtue ethics remind us that morality is not separate from teachers' wider life but is part of their personality. In both teachers' professional ethics and their lives outside the classroom, moral dignity consists primarily not of successful decision making but of responsibility taken for their own character as human beings.

2.3 *Agapism*

Teachers' professional relationship with their students can be described as pedagogical love (Haavio, 1948; Kaukko et al., 2021). One ethical framework that emphasizes love is *agapism*. This approach is based on Christian ethics and posits a binding duty of unconditional love for one's fellow human beings. According to this ethic, all other duties derive from this principal. The ethicist William Frankena (1908–1994) viewed agapism as the third leading ethical framework alongside teleological and deontological ethics (Frankena, 1963, p. 43). From the perspective of a teacher's work, the idea of unconditional love is similar to pedagogical love. Teachers are committed to a student's best interest even if they dislike that student or are ultimately unable to secure that interest. According to Frankena, the ethic of love is highly compatible with the duty of doing good. He presents agapism, augmented with the principals of equality and distributive justice, as an ethical ideal. However, he acknowledges that, as an ethical ideal, it can be striven for but never entirely attained (Frankena, 1963, p. 45).

In teachers' professional ethics we cannot dictate the particular ethical framework and associated ethical principles that a teacher must follow. In the school community, every teacher and student possess their own value base that guides them in their ethical decisions. However, each school community is committed to some shared values that steer its actions. In Finnish schools, the national curriculum and municipality-based and school-based curricula represent such shared values and include the educational goals for schools (FNBE, 2016). School-base curricula allow each school the possibility to define its own values in more detail. Common community values are often those that are seen as valuable from the majority of ethical frameworks.

3 Teachers' Role in Supporting Student Development

When teachers reflect on the best interest of their students, they should consider the ethical basis of their profession. Teaching involves similar problems to those present in other professions. Every profession includes social power that members of the profession must use responsibly. Specialist expertise, status, and authority are common characteristics of each profession. Of these three characteristics, authority can be seen as the most important from an ethical standpoint, as it enables the use of power. However, authority cannot exist without status or skills in the profession (Tirri & Puolimatka, 2000).

In terms of authority, the concept of power is central. However, another crucial aspect is the autonomy or independence of the profession. The value base of the teaching profession emphasizes the holistic development of the student. Teachers' professional competence can be seen as the individual skill to take educational decisions aimed to facilitate that development. In this case, a teacher's professional competence and professional ethics are based on individual authority instead of shared authority (Campbell, 2003). This emphasis on individual authority can be used to justify an individually oriented teacher culture. In such a culture, teachers' professionalism is based on individual decision making where teachers promote the best interest of their students based on their own understanding. Naturally, this requires that teachers' own personal ethics guide their decisions.

In Finland, the ethical nature of the teaching profession includes communality and collegiality (Trade Union of Education in Finland, 2010). Professionally competent teachers can be defined as moral educators who work in collaboration with their colleagues (Sockett, 1993). This emphasis on collegiality is the basis for a multiprofessional collaboration in which adults of the community jointly interpret what is the best interest of their students. In schools, it is important to reflect on the shared ethical principles that guide the community. If teachers agree to commit to collaboration with their colleagues, they also agree to share their authority with other teachers and partners. In schools, members often face conflicts between the interests of different groups. These groups might also display significant differences in the principles that guide the resolution of such conflicts. In these cases, issues related to the ethics of commitment must be addressed (see Section 4 in this chapter).

The power related to membership of a profession offers teachers the possibility to help their students. The challenge in the teaching profession is to motivate students to study and develop their knowledge and skills. It is crucial to guide students to identify their personal goals and the long-term benefits of studying. A teacher can help students by bolstering and improving their external and internal competence. External competence can be related to the concrete organization of studies, for example, finding the right study group or the selection of study materials. By contrast, internal competence involves knowledge and skills, self-confidence and motivation. In helping students develop these competences, the teacher supports the advancement of their agency. For this to be beneficial, both teacher and student must be active. Teaching involves interaction and reciprocity, and, without the active contribution of the student, the goals of teaching cannot be met. Teachers are representatives of their profession and follow the ethical codes of teaching with the aim of achieving the goals defined in the curriculum. Moreover, while teachers act morally in their aim to work for the best interest of their students, their action is not altruistic, as they are paid for their work and can promote their own ambitions while helping their students. Furthermore, while assisting students, teachers retain the right to protect their own privacy and wellbeing (Trade Union of Education in Finland, 2010).

4 Teachers' Commitment to the Profession

The ethics of commitment are based on commitments between people. They include, for example, the commitment between spouses and the commitment between professionals and their clients (Deyhle et al., 1992). The teaching profession's value base, which directs teachers to facilitate the development of the student, is excellently suited to the framework of the ethics of commitment. In the school community, teachers are committed to their students, colleagues and other possible partners. Nevertheless, these many commitments might lead to a conflict of loyalty (Hanhimäki & Tirri, 2009; Tirri & Husu, 2002). Nonetheless, if we define the best interest of students as the goal of education, we can conclude that teachers' commitment to their students is their primary commitment. How then should teachers act in situations where the best interest of different students is in conflict? The central ethical problem in the teaching profession is the interaction between different groups and the conflicts of interest arising from this interaction.

In Finland, the ethical code for teachers and the National Core Curriculum for Basic Education have strongly guided teacher culture to develop in a community-oriented direction. In a community-oriented teacher culture, commitments and shared values are important aspects of discussions about professional ethics. In professional occupations, one way to demonstrate commitment is by swearing an oath of office.

By swearing an oath of office, the novice demonstrates their willingness to commit to the goals and ethical values of the profession. For instance, Medical doctors take the Hippocratic oath during their graduation. In 2017 the Finnish Ethical Committee for the Teaching Profession developed an oath for teachers named Comenius' Oath (Trade Union of Education in Finland 2017, see Table 1), according to the 17th century educational philosopher Johan Comenius (1592–1670). Comenius is viewed as the founder of didactics, and his teaching doctrine is crystallized in the best-known textbook on the topic, the *Didacta Magna*, published in 1657. The English version of this book (Comenius, 1896) is available for download on the Internet.[1]

The goal of Comenius' Oath is to emphasize professional ethics as part of a teacher's professional identity. The Oath emphasizes, for example, a teacher's duty always to act with justice and equality. By taking the Oath, a teacher also

TABLE 1   Comenius' Oath (Trade Union of Education in Finland, 2017)

As a teacher I am engaged in educating the next generation, which is one of the most important human tasks. My aim in this will be to renew and pass on the existing reserve of human knowledge, culture and skills.

I undertake to act with justice and fairness in all that I do and to promote the development of my pupils and students, so that each individual may grow up as a complete human being in accordance with his or her aptitudes and talents. I will also strive to assist parents, guardians and others responsible for working with children and young people in their educational functions.

I will not reveal information that is communicated to me confidentially, and I will respect the privacy of children and young people. I will also protect their physical and psychological inviolability.

I will endeavour to shield the children and young people in my care from political and economic exploitation and defend the rights of every individual to develop his or her own religious and political convictions.

I will make continuous efforts to maintain and develop my professional skills, committing myself to the common goals of my profession and to the support of my colleagues in their work. I will act in the best interest of the community at large and strive to strengthen the esteem in which the teaching profession is held.

---

pledges to advance the development of each student according to their tendencies. Furthermore, a teacher promises to respect the privacy and integrity of children. Finally, the Oath commits teachers to protecting students' right to develop in an environment free from political and economic indoctrination in order to allow them to form their own political and world views. Similar to teachers' ethical code, the Oath is intended for all teachers, from early education to adult education. The Oath, which is an ethical guide without juridical obligations, is aptly suited to educational professionals who work autonomously and who are trusted by society.

5   Questions to Reflect on by Yourself or with Your Peers

- Reflect on the reasons why the teaching profession is more popular in Finland than in other countries. What attracts young people to the teaching profession?
- How does the teaching profession differ from other professions, for example from medicine or law? Reflect also on the similarities between these professions.

– Read the Finnish ethical code for teachers and evaluate them from the following perspectives:
1. Suitability: Are the codes equally suited to all teachers in Finland? Are they suitable for teachers in other countries?
2. Coverage: Is something important missing from the codes? What kind of things are missing? Is there something that could be removed from the codes? What kind of things? Justify your perspectives.
3. Practicality: How can teachers benefit from the codes in their practical work? Provide some examples of such situations. Would it be possible to make the codes more practical? How?
– How can teleological ethics help teachers solve ethically problematic situations in their work?
– What kind of duties do deontological ethics bestow on teachers?
– What do the ethics of commitment mean in teachers' work?
– Are certain types of personalities more suited to teaching than others?
– Describe the characteristics of an ideal teacher. Do you possess them?
– What does teacher authority mean today? Offer some examples from the school context
– How can teachers use power in their profession? Give examples of situations.
– Describe an ideal relationship between a teacher and a colleague. What factors are the most important?
– Describe an ideal relationship between a teacher and a student. How is it possible to create such a relationship?
– Read and carefully consider Comenius' Oath. What are your thoughts on it? Provide both positive and negative perspectives.

Note

1   See https://books.google.com/books/about/The_Great_Didactic_of_John_Amos_Comenius.html?id=sE9MAAAAIAAJ&printsec=frontcover&source=kp_read_button#v=onepage&q&f=false

Ethical Expertise in Teaching

In this chapter, we adhere to the Kohlbergian cognitive school of thought in moral development. We argue that ethical expertise develops through rational thinking and practice. Therefore, it is important for teachers to exercise their skills in principled moral reasoning. In the development of ethical expertise, rules and regulations are important, but their role changes as the teacher's proficiency increases from the slow process of following externally regulated instructions to the fast, automatic implementation of internalized principles that resemble intuition. In distributing justice and solving moral dilemmas, teachers should practice the use of different principles and strategies.

1 The Development of Ethical Expertise

The majority of research related to morality is focused on the development of moral judgment and is based on classic studies by Jean Piaget (1896–1980) and Lawrence Kohlberg (1927–1987) (Piaget, 1965; Kohlberg, 1969). These studies represent cognitive approaches in which morality is studied in the framework of cognitive developmental theories. Kohlberg's moral development theory contains clear stages and is built on the work of Piaget. According to Kohlberg, the highest stage of moral development is reached when a person has developed into an independent agent capable of taking decisions on moral dilemmas based on general principles of justice. Moral thinking is developed deductively, from general principles to individual cases (Tirri, 2003a).

Kohlberg investigated moral judgments by using predefined dilemmas with no obvious right or wrong solution. In his approach, subjects are asked to select the best possible decision in a situation involving conflicting principles of justice. In the original method, these dilemmas were presented in a long interview followed by more detailed questions and a hypothetical situation after the test-taker had taken the decision. After the interview, the answers provided by the subject were analyzed by identifying characteristics typical of Kohlberg's stages, upon which the participant's developmental level of moral thinking was finally decided. Kohlberg formulated a coding system for this analysis that was used for many years in the analysis process. Finally, he created codebook containing standardized coding instructions (Colby & Kohlberg, 1987).

© KONINKLIJKE BRILL NV, LEIDEN, 2022 | DOI:10.1163/9789004532649_003

The cognitive approach has focused on people's conception of justice and its development, which is also one of the goals of moral education (Tirri & Pehkonen, 2002). When teachers and students encounter real-life moral dilemmas, it is important for them to identify the principles that they use to justify their moral arguments. In their work, teachers must find arguments to justify their educational decisions concerning diverse students and teach their students to justify their own moral arguments. In an educational context, the most rational argument should be prioritized in the search for the morally right solution. The teachers' ethical code in Finland emphasizes truthfulness in teachers' ethical conduct. This implies that moral arguments should also be grounded in academic knowledge and research findings.

The importance of truthfulness in teachers' professional ethics is self-evident, as teachers must constantly deal with knowledge and truth. Aiming for the truth can also be seen as the fundamental goal of all education. Moreover, many researchers of the teaching profession cite honesty as one of the basic virtues that enable educators to teach about the good (Clark, 1990, pp. 252–256; Sockett, 1993, pp. 62–88).

Christopher Clark defines truthfulness as speaking the truth and acting in a way that entirely equates with a person's belief in what is true. This definition also includes avoidance of cheating, lying and stealing, plagiarism, and other dishonest acts. In teaching, moral issues with students most often concern truthfulness and cheating (Clark, 1990, p. 253; Tirri, 1999b).

While Kohlberg studied moral development in general, scholars such as Hubert and Stuart Dreyfus focused on development of ethical expertise. They used the analogies of playing chess and driving cars to illustrate the learning of ethical action. In their model, intuition and spontaneity are central aspects of advanced ethical action. In the same way as chess players or drivers learn the rules of the game or the road, teachers learn at least some ethical guidelines within their own community. At first, these guidelines strictly regulate their action, but later they become more context and situation dependent. Once they enter the expert phase of their careers, these rules and regulations provide room for spontaneity (Dreyfus & Dreyfus, 1990).

In practical school life, a teacher's ethical expertise can be defined as the ability to function in an ethically problematic situation as an experienced expert. In chess and driving, the successful result is easy to define. By contrast, in education and teaching the results are seldom seen immediately, and a teacher's success is more difficult to assess. According to the theory proposed by Dreyfus and Dreyfus, ethical expertise is manifested not only as reflection on and adoption of successful principles but in the use of moral intuition. In a problematic situation, ethical experts do not apply certain principles or guidelines; rather they listen and gather information about the case until their intuition guides them to the right decision. Ethical expertise results in fewer ethical problems in practice and tolerance of uncertain situations. However, just as any two experts might have different spontaneous reactions to the same situation, teachers can also react very differently to the unique ethical problems they encounter. In these spontaneous situations, there are often no other guidelines than each teacher's intuition based on earlier experiences of the best action suitable for the situation.

According to the theory proposed by Dreyfus and Dreyfus, ethical expertise is developed through these stages:

1. Novice: Initially, teachers' actions are guided by the rules and regulations of a mentor or the school community, and by following them the novice teacher learns ethical action. New situations without clear rules cause uncertainty for the teacher. In this phase, teachers often feel that they are failing to follow the regulations.

2. Advanced beginner: With experience, a teacher learns to function in different situations. The contexts of these different situations begin to be familiar, and this helps the teacher identify some special characteristics of the problems they encounter.

3. Practiced: Here, teachers use their prior experience to formulate certain hierarchies in their minds regarding problematic ethical situations. Certain situational factors help practiced teachers form a holistic picture of the situation and plan their action. A practiced teacher, however, requires time for analytical thinking to help them understand the holistic nature of the situation and predict future scenarios. This phase includes both successes and failures, with consequent strong emotions.

4. Experienced: The experienced problem identifier and solver abandons slavish adherence to guidelines. The experiences of success and failure in various ethical situations have provided the teacher with a holistic picture of ethical action and related situations. In this phase, the teacher perceives the situation in its entirety and knows how they should act. This action, however, requires careful thinking and planning from the teacher.

5. Expert: The ethical expert is immediately aware of how to act in ethically problematic situations and intuitively acts according to this knowledge. In an ethically problematic situation, the expert functions without the need to consciously consider the requirements of the situation. They do not need to reflect on rules or principles, but nevertheless their actions mirror those in similar situations earlier in their career. This is why they experience fewer ethically problematic situations that demand reflection.

The centrality of intuition in the development of ethical expertise in Dreyfus and Dreyfus's theory might seem similar to 'the new science school of moral psychology' presented, for example, by Joshua Green and Jonathan Haidt (see Damon & Colby, 2015). They claim that moral decisions are based on feelings, intuitions, and neuropsychological responses. However, for Dreyfus and Dreyfus, intuition is not a feeling or emotional response to stimuli but a mature wisdom that is guided by internalized and automatized applied ethical knowledge. Their theory also highlights the importance of deliberate practice and effort in developing expertise in teaching.

2   The Teacher as a Distributor of Justice

An important aspect of teacher ethics is equal treatment of diverse students. For example, students' school achievement and socioeconomic status should not influence teachers' work in educating their students. Schooling, however, involves dilemmas related to teachers' allocation of time and resources to their students (Mäkinen, 2013; Tirri, 1999b). When facing these dilemmas, teachers require support in making ethical decisions. Here, teachers usually turn to ped-agogical principles to support their decision making, but teachers should also reflect on how they can treat different students justly (Kansanen et al., 2000).

In schools, the ideal of inclusion, where diverse students are taught in the same classroom, challenges teachers to reflect on whose needs are primary and whether it is possible to meet all the needs of their students (Tirri & Laine, 2017a, 2017b). Such decision making is demanding, and teachers are not always able to identify the consequences of their actions for their students (Jackson et al., 1993; Tirri et al., 2013). In school communities, teachers should constantly reflect on the values behind their actions. The distributive justice framework emphasizes the need for teachers to behave in an unbiased manner towards different parties in conflicts and situations requiring the distribution of resources. Nevertheless, teachers might hold differing views on what principles to apply in order to treat the people involved in the most just and unbiased manner.

Morton Deutch (1920–2017) defined three possible principles to justify the distribution of resources: equality, equity,[1] and need (Deutch, 1985). In the application of the principle of equality, the teacher aims to share the advantages and disadvantages of a particular situation or action equally among all the parties concerned. In this kind of distributive justice, the teacher acknowledges no inherent differences between parties and considers an unbiased policy to mean 'equality for all.' In turn, by using the principle of equity, teachers compare their students' possible merits or deficiencies and distribute justice based on this comparison. For example, in the application of this principle, the teacher distributes awards and other benefits to those students who have worked or striven the hardest in their studies. However, it is unclear whether the different needs and skills of diverse students are sufficiently considered in this approach. By contrast, when applying the principle of need as the basis of distributing justice, the teacher takes particular care that the needs of different students are acknowledged and met in appropriate ways. Now the teacher advocates policies in which the needs and rights of different kinds of students are secured. For instance, Finland has traditionally taken care of students with learning difficulties or special educational needs. By contrast, high academic achievers have received little special attention from the teacher. However, inclusive education means just education for all, and the teacher is required to acknowledge the needs of gifted students as well, for example, by tailoring instruction to match their level of achievement (Tirri & Laine, 2017a, 2017b).

Kirsi Tirri has investigated the principles of distributive justice used by teachers and students in solving both hypothetical and real-life moral dilemmas (Tirri, 1998, 1999b, 2003a). Her research has identified differences between teachers and students in their use of these principles. For example, in the hypothetical Heinz dilemma, concerning the right to steal medication in order to save a sick person, students tended to apply the principle of need (the sick person needs the drug). Teachers, on the other hand, tended to utilize the principle of equality (stealing is always wrong). However, in real moral dilemmas at school, students used the principles of equality and equity when solving cases related to their teachers and peers. For example, students supported equality in the case of distributing goods and material: all students should receive a similar amount. However, in the case of fighting, students used the principle of equity, since they advocated a harsher punishment for the person who initiated the fight than for others involved. By contrast, students never used the principle of need in these cases. Conversely, teachers most often applied the principle of need to solve real-life moral dilemmas at school. These differences between teachers and students can be explained by their divergent roles. Teachers are guided by their professional ethics and are always primarily committed to serving their students' needs (Tirri, 1998).

A teacher works in a school community comprising colleagues, students and other school staff. In addition, teachers are subject to the expectations of parents and other parties. In school conflicts, teachers should reflect on their solidarity with these different groups. In such situations, teachers generally emphasize their commitment to students and view the principle of acting in the student's best interest as the guiding precept of their work (Tirri, 1999b).

The majority of moral dilemmas at school allow the best interest of the student to be defined in different ways. Moreover, in many disputes, a conflict exists between the best interest of different students. Thus, teachers must decide on the principles of justice they should implement, which can be extremely case specific. This implies that the principles of distributive justice should be reflected in case examples provided to teachers in their pre- and in-service education related to professional ethics.

3   The Teacher as an Ethical Decision-Maker

Teachers' professional morality can be studied using a classical model developed by Fritz Oser (1991) that has been widely used in the Finnish context (Tirri, 1999b, 2021). This model allows teachers' moral dilemmas to be investigated in their natural environment – schools. The model outlines the central dimensions of teachers' professional morality: justice, caring and truthfulness. These dimensions allow reflection from many different perspectives on the moral dilemmas encountered by teachers. The model also recognizes that ethical dilemmas, by nature, seldom have one correct solution. In the teaching profession, the challenge is to search for balanced solutions that accommodate all these dimensions.

In his classic study, Oser (1991) used the terms professional morality and ethos synonymously.[2] The model he constructed discusses the different dimensions of teachers' decision making that must be acknowledged to find the best possible solution (see Figure 1).

According to Oser, moral dilemmas in teaching occur when teachers are unable to balance justice, care, and truthfulness simultaneously. The dimensions presented by Oser are very similar to the values underpinning Finnish

FIGURE 1   Dimensions of the teachers' ethos model (adapted from Oser, 1991, p. 202)

teachers' ethical principles. The challenge for teachers is to find solutions that take all of these dimensions into account in decision making. In Oser's theory, teachers can apply five different types of orientations in moral dilemmas: *avoiding, delegating, single-handed decision making, discourse I*, and *discourse II*. In the avoiding orientation, teachers strive to solve the problem by ignoring it. They are unwilling to take responsibility for difficult questions and leave the task of balancing between justice, caring, and truthfulness to others. In turn, teachers with a *delegating orientation* accept their obligations concerning the moral dilemma in question. However, they are reluctant to take decisions themselves and instead delegate decision making to others (for example, colleagues, parents, the principal) In a *single-handed decision-making orientation*, teachers attempt to solve the situation by themselves. Here, teachers view themselves as authorities in problem solving, and thus see no need to justify their decisions to anybody. According to Oser, moral dilemmas require discourse orientations. In an *incomplete discourse orientation*, teachers discuss the dilemma with the others involved and justify the principles they used in solving moral dilemmas. They trust that their students are also capable of reflecting on these justifications. Oser advocates a *complete discourse orientation*, in which teachers treat each party equally and allow all those involved to argue and justify their perspectives. In this orientation, the final decision is determined by the rationality of the best argument (Oser, 1992, p. 112). Nonetheless, this kind of orientation is extremely challenging and time consuming for the teachers, since some situations can involve aggression or be impossible to solve.

4   The Teacher as an Ethical Discussant

In every working community, common rules and the rights of minorities must be discussed. In the current community-oriented teacher culture, where the ethics of commitment are emphasized, the skills to discuss ethical issues become central. However, some 20 years ago, at the beginning of the 21st century, teachers from different grade levels already highlighted the need to discuss various themes in their own communities. The most important of these included the community's vision, power and leadership, the tension between individuality and communality, and issues related to commitment (Tirri, 2002).

When striving to create communality, it is important that each member is able to present their view of the current issues affecting the community. In Oser's adaptation of Habermas' discourse ethics model to the context of schools (Oser, 1986; Habermas, 1984), the only requirement for participation is the readiness to adopt the role of the other and provide the opportunity for everybody to be heard. In order to understand the situation, participants in the discussion must be aware of the needs and motives of the people involved, understand their life situations and know the rules that apply to the situation (Oser, 1986, p. 921). Kirsi Tirri has further developed the model for use in Finnish schools and teacher education. She calls it a 'roundtable discussion' and suggests that it should include 'a critical friend' from outside school who brings an objective perspective to the discussion. Such critical friends can be, for example, church workers, police youth workers, social workers or partners cooperating with the school (Tirri, 2003b). Figure 2 presents the roundtable discussion, in which the current ethical issues, such as inclusive education, can be discussed.

In the following case example, the teacher arranges a roundtable discussion in school to discuss a situation in the context of their 4th grade mathematics class. The teacher currently teaches 30 students with different mathematical skills and motivation in the same classroom. The majority of students ($n = 17$) are average math learners: they experience no major difficulties in the subject, but they require instruction from the teacher when new topics are presented. In turn, three students are high achievers and already master the entire 4th grade math curriculum. By contrast, two students are frustrated and bored and spend most of their time sleeping during the lessons; moreover, one of them frequently disturbs other students and prevents them from listening. The teacher attempts to engage this student by using him as her teaching assistant, with unsatisfactory results. Three students have an immigrant background and lack sufficient Finnish skills to follow the teacher's instruction. One student has down syndrome and faces consequent physical and cognitive challenges. This student is normally supported by a personal assistant, but the assistant is

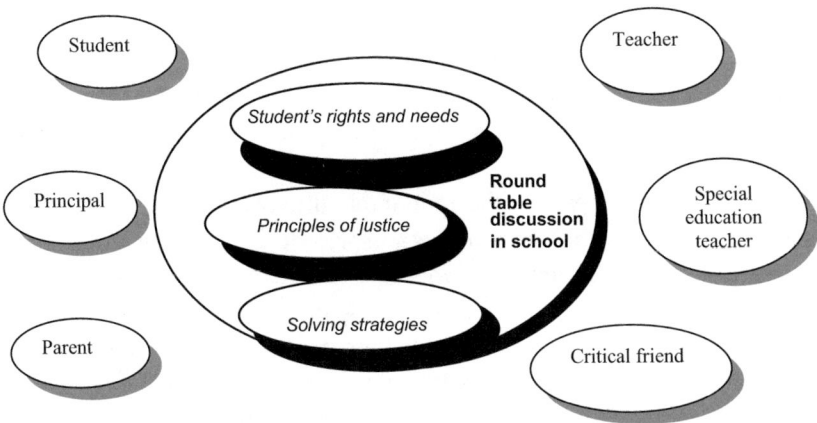

FIGURE 2 Roundtable discussion in school

currently on sick leave. The rest of the students ($n = 6$) are, for different reasons, low math achievers, and they use their time disturbing each other. The teacher wishes to discuss who they should prioritize in the math class and how they should divide their time and resources between different learners.

In this roundtable discussion, the teacher has invited members of the school community (the principal, a special education teacher, a student representative, and a parent representative) and a critical friend (a senior teacher from another school specialized in special education). The principal has booked a meeting room with a round table where the discussion can take place after school hours. The teacher acts as the chair of the discussion and is responsible for ensuring that everyone can be heard. In the meeting invitation, the teacher has described the problem related to their mathematics classes in a very concrete way. They require support and advice on how to meet the needs of different learners in the same classroom.

The teacher opens the discussion by emphasizing that every student has the right to learn in school. The teacher then asks how this could be realized in a classroom with diverse students, and what kind of principles and solutions can be identified. The student and parent representatives as well as the principal and special education teacher bring their perspectives to the discussion on students' rights and needs in their school. The critical friend, in turn, provides approaches to the discussion on how such matters have been successfully addressed in a neighborhood school with a similar student population.

In a case such as this, the roundtable participants might prioritize different groups in their arguments and disagree on whose rights and needs are the most important. Thus, reflection on the principles of justice is essential. In this case, the principle of need guides the discussion. The aim is to identify ways to meet the needs of the majority as well as those of the immigrant students, high achieving students, low achieving students, and the disabled student. All the members provide their suggestions and ideas to reach this goal. In a situation involving conflicting perspectives, the most educationally robust option is chosen. A critical friend can, for example, attempt to reconcile the differences that arise in these discussions.

A practical requirement for the roundtable discussion is the readiness of each member to adopt the role of others and provide the opportunity for them to be heard. Utilizing this approach advances responsibility, justice and social learning for everybody involved. A roundtable discussion is an example of a situation where teachers can relinquish their traditional role as an authority figure and offer equal opportunities for students and other partners to express their views. This requires teachers to change their attitude and strategies. Teachers must adopt an attitude of trust towards all participants in the discussion to be able to search for a solution that includes justice, caring and truthfulness. Teachers must also possess the skills to organize the discussion in such a way that they are simultaneously participants and leaders. Teachers require the skill to balance and coordinate the different views of individuals. Most importantly, however, teachers must trust, in advance, that the discussion will ultimately provide the best solution and that a joint decision is preferable to a unilateral one (Oser & Althof, 1993).

Teachers can accustom their students to roundtable discussions, argumentation and debate by using hypothetical situations or cases of problematic situations identified by the students. School communities can arrange roundtable discussions with different members. In issues concerning the entire school community, each class can send a representative, and the teachers' union and parents' association can also send theirs. From an educational perspective, roundtable discussions support argumentation skills and social learning and strengthen moral responsibility (Tirri, 1999b). In the best cases, roundtable discussions become a natural way to solve conflicts in the everyday life of schools and build a shared vision of the future of the school and its classes.

5   Questions to Reflect on by Yourself or with Your Peers

- How do novice teachers and experienced teachers differ from each other? Reflect on the question based on your own experiences.
- Is it possible for ethical action to be intuitive and spontaneous, or is rational thinking required? Compare these perspectives and take your own stand on this matter.
- What kind of teacher is a just teacher? Discuss this with your peers and compare your views.
- How can teachers distribute their time with justice in teaching both slow learners and fast learners in the same class? Present some pedagogical options.
- Whose needs are primary for the teacher in inclusive education? Why?
- How is caring manifested in a teacher's professional work? Provide some examples based on your own experiences.
- In what kinds of situations does a teacher need to reflect on truthfulness? Is it possible that truthfulness prevents caring in some situations? Think about some example situations.
- What kind of issues should be discussed more in school communities? Why?

- What kind of readiness should teachers have for ethical discussions in schools? How can these skills be learned?
- Practice a roundtable discussion in a group. Divide the roles so that somebody is a teacher and the others are students and parents. Include a critical friend in the discussion. Discuss the themes in Figure 2.

Notes

1   The OECD (Field et al., 2007) has defined equity as inclusion, indicating that a basic minimum standard of education is guaranteed to all, and as fairness, meaning that socio-economic barriers to education are reduced. Further, in the current discussion on inclusion, the word 'equity' has become the prevailing concept and has sometimes even replaced 'equality' (for more, see Tirri & Kuusisto, 2022).
2   Oser's more recent work discusses the possible differences between professional morality and professional ethos, the former referring to supporting students' learning and latter to students' holistic development (Oser & Biedermann, 2018).

Ethical Sensitivity in Teaching

In the previous chapter, we adhered to Kohlberg's cognitive tradition in moral development by emphasizing rationality in teachers' moral argumentation and justification for their ethical conduct. In our research on teachers' professional morality, we have adapted Oser's ethos model to include caring as an important aspect of ethical reflection. This chapter discusses caring as part of the ethical sensitivity that teachers require to identify moral dilemmas in their work and predict the consequences of different solutions to these dilemmas. Moreover, teachers require tools to assess their own and their students' skills in ethical sensitivity. In this chapter, we present a self-report instrument that can be used in educational contexts in different cultures.

1 Caring in Teachers' Professional Ethics

Moral thinking that emphasizes empathy and caring assigns priority to human relationships when solving moral dilemmas. Genuine encounters with others and protection of the weak are the most important aspects of the search for right actions. Hypothetical moral dilemmas used in Kohlberg's studies are dominated by authoritative relationships and ownership. Reflection on these dilemmas develop students' cognitive thinking and the search for universal principles of justice. By contrast, the real-life moral dilemmas that young people encounter are dominated by social and romantic relationships (Tirri, 2003a). In real-life moral dilemmas, people encounter, in addition to questions of justice, many other factors that influence their decisions. A person's moral decision making is not guided by abstract rational thinking; rather affective factors are also influential, including devotion and emotional ties (Bandura, 1991; Rest, 1983). Moreover, instead of reaching decisions deductively, the person often reflects on the specifics of the individual case. Nevertheless, moral thinking can be inductive and the right action determined case by case. In human relationships, empathy and adopting the role of the other person are skills that provide a wider perspective for solving moral dilemmas than does the search for a logical and just decision alone. Interestingly, gender differences have been found between the choice of a justice-oriented or care-oriented solution, with males tending to favor universal justice-oriented thinking and females more likely to adopt a care-oriented approach (Gilligan & Attanucci, 1988).

Nel Noddings is one of the main advocates of caring in teacher-student relationships. Ideal caring requires deep empathy and commitment from a teacher. Teachers need to constantly nurture caring in their work with dialogue and model learning. According to Noddings, this kind of ethical caring is rooted in our biological and psychological structures and based on the natural sympathy we feel for each other (Noddings, 1984, 1992).

In a caring relationship, a person wishes to do good for the other, understands them and their life situation and is prepared to strive for their best interest. Nevertheless, a teacher cannot act or make decisions on behalf of a student. They can simply highlight the student's potential to develop. This kind of care is emancipatory in nature and is intended to help students find their own path.

In sum, mature solutions to moral dilemmas require ethical sensitivity and care in addition to a well-developed conception of justice. Thus, justice can be viewed as a necessary but insufficient condition of a moral system. A brutal person can be just or completely biased in their brutality. By contrast, a society that connects the principle of justice to care is much more of a truly human community than a society pursuing justice alone (Peters, 1966).

2   What Is Ethical Sensitivity?

As society grows ever more diverse, teachers require ethical sensitivity to interact with different partners. A teacher needs the skill to adopt the role of diverse students, families and colleagues when reflecting on shared goals and aims. Ethical sensitivity means awareness of the way our actions affect other people (Bebeau et al., 1999). Without ethical sensitivity, it is impossible for a teacher to identify ethical challenges in the school community. A teacher with ethical sensitivity skills can identify the ethical issues present in different situations and visualize multiple options for solving them. Ethical expertise consists of four different skills: ethical sensitivity, ethical judgment, ethical motivation, and ethical action (Bebeau et al., 1999; Narvaez & Endicott, 2009). In teachers' professional ethics, ethical sensitivity is a key factor for identifying and solving moral dilemmas in schools. Without recognizing the ethical dimension in education, ethical questions cannot proceed to decision making and ethical action.

Narvaez and Endicott (2009; Narvaez, 2001) operationalize ethical sensitivity in terms of seven skills: (1) reading and expressing emotions, (2) adopting the perspective of others, (3) caring by connecting to others, (4) working with interpersonal and group differences, (5) preventing social bias, (6) generating interpretations and options, and (7) identifying the consequences of action and options. We have developed the Ethical Sensitivity Scale Questionnaire (ESSQ, see Table 2) to provide self-assessment tools for teachers' and students (Tirri & Nokelainen, 2011).

TABLE 2   Ethical Sensitivity Scale Questionnaire (ESSQ)

Dimensions		Items	
1	Reading and expressing emotions	es1_1	In conflict situations, I am able to identify other people's feelings.
		es1_2	I am able to express my different feelings to other people.
		es1_3	I notice if someone working with me is offended by me.
		es1_4	I am able to express to other people if I am offended or hurt because of them.
2	Taking the perspectives of others	es2_5[a]	I am able to cooperate with people who do not share my opinions on what is right and what is wrong.
		es2_6[a]	I tolerate different ethical views in my surroundings.
		es2_7[a]	I think it is good that my closest friends think in different ways.
		es2_8[a]	I also get along with people who do not agree with me.
3	Caring by connecting to others	es3_9[a]	I am concerned about the wellbeing of my partners.
		es3_10[a]	I take care of the wellbeing of others and try to improve it.
		es3_11[a]	In conflict situations, I do my best to take actions that aim at maintaining good personal relationships.
		es3_12[a]	I try to have good contact with all the people I am working with.
4	Working with interpersonal and group differences	es4_13	I take other people's points of view into account before making any important decisions in my life.
		es4_14	I try to consider another person's position when I face a conflict situation.
		es4_15[a]	When I am working on ethical problems, I consider the impact of my decisions on other people.
		es4_16	I try to consider other people's needs, even in situations concerning my own benefits.
5	Preventing social bias	es5_17	I recognize my own bias when I take a stand on ethical issues.
		es5_18	I realize that I am tied to certain prejudices when I assess ethical issues.
		es5_19	I try to control my own prejudices when making ethical evaluations.
		es5_20	When I am resolving ethical problems, I try to take a position evolving out of my own social status.

(cont.)

TABLE 2   Ethical Sensitivity Scale Questionnaire (ESSQ) (*cont.*)

Dimensions	Items	
6 Generating interpretations and options	es6_21[a]	I contemplate the consequences of my actions when making ethical decisions.
	es6_22[a]	I ponder different alternatives when aiming at the best possible solution to an ethically problematic situation.
	es6_23	I am able to create many alternative ways to act when I face ethical problems in my life.
	es6_24[a]	I believe there are several right solutions to ethical problems.
7 Identifying the consequences of actions and options	es7_25[a]	I notice that there are ethical issues involved in human interaction.
	es7_26[a]	I see a lot of ethical problems around me.
	es7_27[a]	I am aware of the ethical issues I face at school.
	es7_28[a]	I am better than other people at recognizing new and current ethical problems.

a   Items used in this book since they have been found to be the most valid in different datasets from different cultures (see Gholami et al., 2015; Ronkainen et al., 2021).

Instruments like the EESQ are required to study ethical sensitivity in teaching. Currently there are 20 different tools measuring ethical sensitivity of which three are designed for teachers and educational contexts (Brabeck et al., 2000; Maxwell et al., 2021; Tirri & Nokelainen, 2007, 2011). Measuring ethical sensitivity is challenging. It requires rigorous development of the instrument by critically estimating the validity and reliability of the scale. Therefore, many participants and answers are required for this iterative process. When developing an instrument, it is essential that items measure what they are intended to measure and that they capture the theoretically identified phenomenon and its structure. Our studies indicate an overlap and strong correlation between some of Narvaez's dimensions. Thus, we have crystallized ethical sensitivity into four dimensions in the context of teaching: 1) Reading ethical issues, 2) Identifying the consequences of actions and options, 3) Taking the perspective of others and 4) Caring by connecting to others (Gholami et al., 2015; Ronkainen et al., 2021). This means that an ethically sensitive person is able to see the ethical nature of situations and can visualize the possible implications of actions and statements. Such individuals are also able adopt the perspectives of others and wish to care for their wellbeing.

2.1   *Ethical Sensitivity in Different Cultures*

As a concept and phenomenon, ethical sensitivity was first acknowledged in the US (Rest, 1985; Narvaez & Endicott, 2009). However, when a theory or model has been developed in one country, it is important to study, test and validate it in other cultures and countries. In this section, we present our research on identifying the culture-dependent and culture-independent features of ethical sensitivity. We investigated the relationship between the dimensions of ethical sensitivity and the structure of the phenomenon in three different countries: Finland, Estonia and Iran (Gholami et al., 2015; Ronkainen et al., 2021).

A study conducted by Hofsted, Hoftsted and Minkov (2010) on cultural differences identified five dimensions that distinguish various countries. These dimensions are individuality-collectivity, power distance, indulgence-restraint, long term-short term orientation and masculinity-femininity. Table 3 presents the cultural dimensions that characterize the countries we have studied. Finland and Estonia both represent European cultures that emphasize individuality and equality (Hofstede et al., 2010). By contrast, Iranian culture emphasizes collectivity, large power distances (e.g., the teacher is an explicit authority) and strict social norms influenced by the Iranian interpretation of Islam. In turn, Finnish and Iranian cultures value virtues related to the past and present, which can be seen in appreciation of education and moral education in schools. Instead, Estonian culture emphasizes virtues directed towards the future and economic success, such as persistence and frugality. From the perspective of education, this has meant that in Estonia moral education has not been seen as integral part of school pedagogy until recently. However, these three countries all share a feminist approach in the sense that all people are expected to be interested in human relations and the quality of life.

The participants in our studies were Finnish teachers (n = 864, of which 522 were in-service teachers and 342 were preservice), Estonian teachers (n = 412) and Iranian teachers (n = 556). All three groups ranked highly in ethical sensitivity, which can be explained by teaching being viewed as a deeply ethical

TABLE 3   Cultural dimensions of Finland, Estonia and Iran

Cultural dimensions	Finland	Estonia	Iran
Individualism-collectivism	Individualism	Individualism	Collectivism
Power distance	Small	Small	Large
Indulgence-restraint	Indulgence	Restraint	Restraint
Long term-short term orientation	Short	Long	Short
Masculinity-femininity	Femininity	Femininity	Femininity

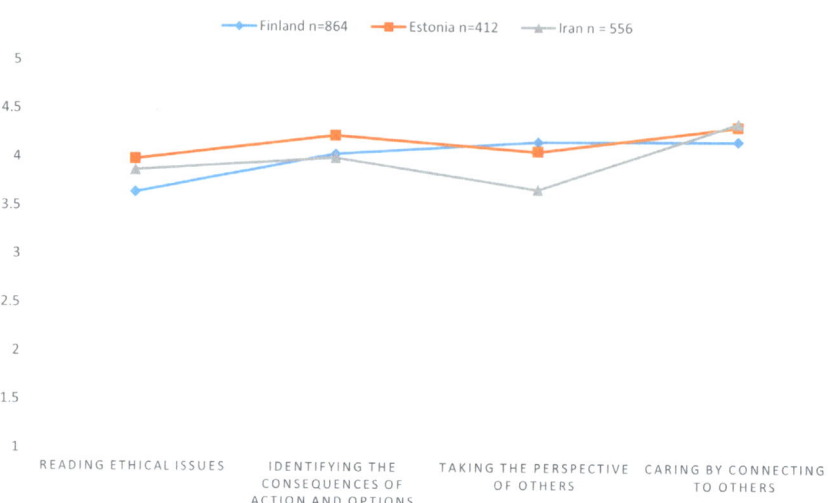

FIGURE 3   Ethical sensitivity among Finnish, Estonian and Iranian teachers

profession in these countries. By contrast, the Iranian teachers scored lower than their Finnish and Estonian counterparts on adopting the perspective of others, a result that is connected to the collective features of Iranian culture, where communal perspectives override those of the individual. In all three countries, teachers scored the highest for caring by connecting to others and the lowest for reading ethical issues (Figure 3).

Taking the perspective of others was found to be a culturally dependent dimension of ethical sensitivity. In Finland and Estonia, *taking the perspective of others* predicted caring for others, indicating that in Finnish and Estonian cultures caring means an empathetical approach where one attempts to view the world through the eyes of others or places oneself 'in their shoes.' Instead, in Iran *taking the perspective of others* was neither directly nor indirectly associated with caring for others, which indicates that in Iran Islamic and collectivistic values are prioritized over the values and thoughts of individuals. This can also be seen in Iranian teacher education, where only confessional Muslims who are committed to advocating the religious values of society are chosen for teacher education (Hedayati et al., 2017b).

Ethical sensitivity is manifested in different cultures and countries in different ways. However, *caring by connecting to others* seems to represent the core of ethical sensitivity regardless of culture or country. It is manifested in concern and taking care about wellbeing of others and keeping good relations even in conflict situations. Our empirical results about teachers' ethical sensitivity in different countries indicate that ethical sensitivity is understood in same ways in different countries, however, teachers can emphasize different aspects of ethical sensitivity in their work. Empirical findings also support the culture invariant nature of the definition of ethical sensitivity we have used.

3   Ethical Sensitivity in Identifying and Solving Moral Dilemmas in Schools

Acknowledging the dimensions of ethical sensitivity helps teachers identify their existing strengths and areas requiring further development. In teaching, ethical sensitivity is necessary for identifying and solving moral dilemmas. Moreover, in multicultural schools, the different backgrounds of students, teachers and parents challenge us to build a shared school culture that values and understands diversity.

3.1   *Teachers' and Students' Perspectives*
In addition to quantitative studies, we have explored teachers' and students' skills in identifying moral dilemmas and conflicts with qualitative approaches. In a recent study conducted in Tehran, Iran, 20 teachers were interviewed, and 302 secondary school students wrote essays about moral conflicts in their schools (Hedayati et al., 2019). The data included 163 girls from a female school and 139 boys from a male school. In both schools, 10 female and 10 male teachers participated. Here, data collection replicated Tirri's (1999b, 2003a) earlier studies: the teachers were asked to describe the most challenging moral dilemma they had experienced in their work, while students were advised to write stories about unfair situations in school. 40 students were then interviewed about their stories.

Matters related to staff behavior comprised the largest category of moral conflict in Iranian schools (Table 4). This category includes issues related to the behavior of teachers, principals and assistant principals. Punishment was the most common theme of moral conflicts identified by students, including stories related to unfair and aggressive sanctions. The following example from a female student illustrates a conflict related to aggressive punishment, which in this case was physical:

> One of our teachers is very aggressive. She does not care about students. Once, two of my friends were talking in class, and the teacher hit their hands with a ruler .... We were sad. (Iranian female student, Hedayati et al., 2019, p. 6)

By contrast, no Iranian teacher identified punishment as a moral dilemma in their school. However, in a previous study on moral dilemmas in Finnish

TABLE 4   Moral conflicts in Iranian schools (from Hedayati et al., 2019, p. 6)

Moral conflicts	Students' perspective		Teachers' perspective	
	Female	Male	Female	Male
	$n = 163$	$n = 139$	$n = 10$	$n = 10$
	f	f	f	f
Matters related to staff behavior	120	128	8	2
Punishment	94	106		
Other matters	26	22	8	2
Matters related to student behavior	101	120	2	2
Students' work ethic	67	68	2	2
Peer relations	34	52		
Sensitive issues	15			2
Matters related to religion	15			1
Matters related to minorities				1
Matters related to parent behavior	2		3	4

schools, teachers indeed identified punishment as an important ethical issue related to their work (Tirri, 1999b). In Finland, such punishment refers to detention and notes to parents, which are currently delivered more and more with digital communication tools (Kuusimäki et al., 2019). Even though the physical punishment of students is forbidden in both countries, there seems to be a distinct cultural difference in the application of this rule (Hedayati et al., 2019, Österman et al., 2014). In Finnish schools, physical punishment has been forbidden since 1914, and corporal punishment in society at large has been prohibited since 1984 (Österman et al., 2014; Wikipedia, 2021). In Finland, teachers' ethical code and Comenius' Oath both acknowledge the importance of protecting students' physical and psychological inviolability. While Iranian teachers rank high in self-assessed ethical sensitivity (Gholami et al., 2015), especially in caring by connecting to others, the reports of students from Iranian schools nevertheless show that caring does not seem to manifest in their teaching behavior.

The second largest category among Iranian teachers and students concerned matters related to students' behavior. This category included issues related to students' work ethic and peer relations. The same issues had already been identified in Tirri's (1999b, 2003a) studies in Finland. In both countries, problems in students' work ethic refer to cheating, insulting language and neglection of homework and study tasks. In turn, harassment was the most commonly mentioned challenge in peer relations in both countries. A study by Tirri (2003a) found that in Finland 50% of the conflicts concerned harassment (Tirri, 2003a), which is surprising, since Finnish schools have adopted a zero tolerance policy against all bullying.

Finnish schools have widely implemented the anti-bullying program KiVa-school (Salmivalli, 2010; Salmivalli et al., 2011), that provides tools and materials for schools to prevent bullying. However, despite achieving some promising results, the programme has thus far failed to solve this challenge. The current educational policy in Finland attempts to criminalize bullying in schools and hold students accountable for their actions (Finnish Parliament, 2020; Vierimaa, 2012). An interesting cross-cultural difference regarding moral conflicts in Iranian and Finnish schools seems to be that aggressive behavior in Iran was mostly related to adults' behavior, while in Finland it concerned students' behavior.

Sensitive issues in Iranian schools were related to religion, ethnicity and sexual relations (Hedayati et al., 2017a, 2019). The same topics were also included in moral dilemmas identified by Finnish teachers (Tirri 1999b), even though the Finnish constitution guarantees equal rights and non-discrimination for all, irrespective of gender, age, ethnicity, language, religion, worldview, opinion, health, or disability (Finnish Constitution 731/1999). Finnish teachers' ethical code emphasize dignity and 'respect for humanity.' According to the code, '[t]eachers must respect every person, regardless of gender, sexual orientation, gender diversity, appearance, age, religion, social standing, origin, opinions, abilities and achievements' (Trade Union of Education in Finland, 2010), indicating an even broader perspectives than the constitution.

Matters related to parents' behavior were also identified as a source of moral conflicts in Iranian schools. Teachers reported that parents failed to cooperate with the school or asked teachers to assign their children better grades than they deserved (Hedayati et al., 2019). In Finnish studies, early education and elementary school teachers reported similar moral dilemma with Finnish parents related to cooperation. In many cases, parents ended their collaboration with teachers or removed the child from kindergarten if they disliked their educational practices (Tirri & Husu, 2002). In the following example, a kindergarten teacher describes a moral dilemma she had encountered with parents in her work:

> I have a child in my kindergarten group who is developmentally delayed in many areas. This is a very difficult thing for his parents to admit. We

have tried to discuss this issue with them with a medical doctor, but these discussions have not changed their attitude. The child should start school in a year and a half, but I don't think he is mature enough for it. Every time I talk with his parents, I feel I am torturing them with suggestions of speech therapy, etc. However, I didn't think I had a choice here. I told the parents that their child needs professional help in order to be ready for school. The parents were very angry with me, and they told me they would transfer their child to another kindergarten. Their cooperation with me was finished. I knew I did the right thing because I had the support of my supervisor and colleagues. I had to take the perspective of the child even it did not please his parents. I had to be honest with the parents. Now it is their choice what to do with their child. I could only suggest ways to help the child develop. (Finnish kindergarten teacher, Tirri & Husu, 2002, pp. 70–71)

Teachers' professional ethics are guided by truthfulness manifested in honesty in communication with parents. Teachers cannot raise grades or evaluate students based on parental expectations. According to Finnish studies, moral issues in schools are not always solved in a positive way. Discussions and consultations often fail to cause improvement, and cases frequently remain open and unsolved (Tirri & Husu, 2002). However, in these negotiations with parents, students and colleagues, teachers can demonstrate that they are caring, responsible and ethical professionals.

3.2   *Parents' Perspectives*
We have extended our studies on parents to involve a European country, Portugal, where collectivity in education is emphasized (Levinthal et al., 2021). In our study Finnish (n = 10) and Portuguese (n = 9) parents were interviewed about their perspectives on how teachers can support the parent-teacher partnership and parental engagement in school (see Table 5). In both countries, parents expected good communication from teachers to support the teacher-parent partnership. According to parents, a teacher should be able to engage in dialogue with parents about their children's education. In such dialogue, the teacher should be able to adopt the perspective of the parents and be emotionally easy to approach. Ethical sensitivity provides teachers with more opportunities for success in this dialogue, as the following example from a Finnish father illustrates:

The most important component is smooth communication and no barrier. Because if you don't have a barrier, you can also approach the teacher with some problematic issues or ask for advice …. We all are emotional

TABLE 5   Parents' perspectives on how teachers can support the parent-teacher partnership
(from Levinthal et al., 2021, p. 8)

Teachers support partnership and parental engagement when they ...	Finnish (*n* = 10) *f*	Portuguese (*n* = 9) *f*	Total (N = 19) *f*
Communicate	76	59	135
Engage in dialogue	42	34	76
Inform	26	12	38
Give pedagogical advice	7	4	11
Welcome parents' initiatives	1	9	10
Show professionalism	44	24	68
Have competence to teach	38	17	55
Have a good pedagogical relationship with the child	6	7	13
Invite active participation	27	28	55
Invite participation in parental activities	15	26	41
Invite participation in collaborative activities	12	2	14
Total of statements	147	111	258

beings, and we see things in a different way, so it is important to communicate, to speak things out and to be understood. (Finnish father, Levinthal et al., 2021, p. 9)

Teachers also require ethical sensitivity to understand when parents require more information about their child's schooling. In the following, a Finnish mother explains her needs related to teacher-parent communication:

It is very important information to me because my son doesn't speak so much. I ask him how the day was, and (he answers) 'it was good.' I am left wondering about what is happening in real life, because I can't be there watching what's happening, so it's the only way to get the information. I like to get these emails. (Finnish mother, Levinthal et al., 2021, p. 9)

The parents in this study also mentioned their expectations of teachers' professional behavior, manifested in their competence to teach and in a good pedagogical relationship with the child. In the following quote, a Finnish father discusses the professional behavior that he values:

It is also the motivation you can see in the teacher, how dedicated they are to the class. Like, how often they change a group or school. Sometimes, if there's some trouble for the school to have a motivated teacher stay with the group for a long time, you can see that they change the teacher every half a year. But, sometimes, you have a teacher that stays for many years, and it makes a big difference to get to know the teacher. Also that they have a long period of time with your child, so they get to know them personally and see the growth, and also have an effect on their learning skills, and if there's some problems, they can address them and see the results. (Finnish father, Levinthal et al., 2021, p. 10)

In Finland, teachers are ethical professionals with both pedagogical and ethical competence. Ethical professionalism includes ethical codes and academic education. By contrast, Portuguese teachers lack an explicit ethical code; thus, contrary to their Finnish counterparts, they cannot be regarded as ethical professionals. This aspect was also evident in the interviews with Portuguese parents, where less emphasis was placed on teacher professionalism (Levinthal et al., 2021).

Both Finnish and Portuguese parents emphasized the importance of teachers' invitations to parents to participate actively in school. However, Finnish parents highlighted collaborative activities more than did their Portuguese peers. In the current Finnish educational climate, parents are regarded as members of the school learning community and important partners in developing schools.

All the activities where my engagement is bigger involves organizing, with other parents, all these activities besides school. It's about social engagement with other parents. The way the teacher has managed that is really good. She took on a very big responsibility, kind of drew all the parents in. We have this small group of parents who organize this event in the spring, kevätkeikaus. It's kind of a big event, a lot of parents go there and all different classes that they (the school) have. So, the teacher took care of the responsibility and let us do that, and we just did it. And it's good we have those [events] because it is not only about having a relationship with the teacher, but socializing, having this relationship with the other parents. (Finnish father, Levinthal et al., 2021, p. 11)

In Finnish schools, parental associations are a crucial element in increasing collaboration between teachers and parents as well cooperation among parents. The role of principals in school in creating the atmosphere and culture for cooperation between different parties.

3.3   *Principals' Perspectives*

Our recent qualitative multiple case study involving four school leaders from Estonia and Finland investigated the current ethical challenges principals identify in developing their schools (Tirri et al., 2021). The principals were deliberately chosen for the study, as they had been acknowledged as exemplar school leaders who were respected by their peers, collaborated with universities and were committed to developing their schools and their leadership skills. In the interviews, four topics were discussed: the interviewee's role as a principal, pedagogical interaction in school, curriculum development and pedagogical leadership.

As Table 6 shows, principals identified the development of the learning community as the greatest challenge in both countries. This theme included issues related to teacher collaboration, cooperation with families, student engagement, the wellbeing of learning community members, and cooperation with external partners.

The challenge of teacher collaboration stems from the history of educational systems and teacher education. In Estonia and Finland, elementary school teachers and secondary school teachers are educated separately in

TABLE 6   Categories of current challenges identified by Finnish and Estonian principals (from Tirri et al., 2021, p. 6)

Categories and themes	Finnish (n = 2) f	Estonian (n = 2) f
Learning community development:	17	26
Teacher collaboration	6	7
Cooperation with families	4	6
Student engagement	0	4
Well-being of LC members	3	6
Cooperation with external members	4	3
Curriculum development	16	14
Inclusive education	8	3
ICT	2	2
Assessment	3	3
Phenomenon-based learning	1	4
Learning environment	2	2
Principals' professional development	9	8
Total of statements	42	48

their own programs. Elementary school teachers (class teachers of grades 1–6) graduate with a masters' degree in education, while secondary school teachers (subject teachers of grades 7–9) graduate with a master's degree in their subject, for example mathematics or English language (Tirri, 2014). However, in both countries, teachers in basic education (grades 1–9) work in the same learning community and even in the same physical buildings. Traditionally, teacher culture has been individually oriented, with an emphasis on teacher autonomy, indicating that teachers have not collaborated with each other. However, the current educational policy calls for the development of learning communities, which demands collaboration between teachers of different grade levels and subjects.

Both Estonian and Finnish principals identified the same challenge concerning collaboration between class teachers and subject teachers, indicating the need to educate teachers in ethical sensitivity, especially in the domain of adopting the perspective of others. Here, it seems that it is easier to adopt the perspective of teachers with similar rather than different educational backgrounds. Differences in status and salary create circumstances where teachers mostly identify themselves with those of parallel standing. In the following example, a female Estonian principal describes this challenge:

> At first, we had this hierarchical arrogance … the teacher in a high school thought that teachers in elementary schools should be paid less, not to mention the other benefits. Also, the teachers in elementary schools said, well, it is easy to be a teacher in first grade; think about how hard our work is … now for four years, we have had these learning communities comprising teachers of different subjects at different levels, who meet regularly twice a month … after half a year, we asked the teachers what they thought and what we found … and there is much more respect for and trust in colleagues. (Kadri, Tartu, Estonia, Tirri et al., 2021, pp. 4–5)

This Estonian principal has thus been able to improve teacher collaboration in her school through frequent teacher meetings.

The male Finnish principal of a multicultural school in the next quote had attempted to create collaboration among elementary and secondary teachers for decades. Here, he describes the process and his vision for the comprehensive school.

> The challenge of building a comprehensive school that started in 1996, the ideology of the comprehensive school, still divides teachers. Teachers

at elementary schools and secondary schools are still too far from each other, and we cannot build our learning community with this kind of separation. We have worked on this challenge in this school more than in many other schools, and I have not given up on this ideology and development. I can discuss many issues, and we take different ideas to the school board and discuss them, but this ideology of the comprehensive school is something on which I cannot compromise. (Jaakko, Helsinki, Finland, Tirri et al., 2021, p. 5)

This principal had tried several strategies over the years but had come to conclusion that the effective solution was changing the physical learning environment to support and even force teachers to work together.

The second most mentioned challenge was related to curriculum development. This category included challenges related to inclusive education, ICT, assessment, phenomenon-based learning and the learning environment. In Finland, the current policy of inclusive education presents a challenge to teaching and learning in classrooms. In a multicultural school with 38 spoken languages and over 50% of students with an immigrant background, the language of communication becomes a central issue, as described below:

We are very close to a situation in which we do not have a Finnish-speaking population in our school. This means that learning about the Finnish language and culture is much slower and more difficult. The knowledge does not come from inside the learning community, it comes from outside. It is very important to maintain good co-operative relationships with actors from the different cultures and groups in order to help these multicultural students in their learning. (Jaakko, Helsinki, Finland, Tirri et al., 2021, p. 6)

Even though it is important to meet the needs of multicultural families and respect different cultures, schools must also provide the necessary skills in Finnish language and cultural heritage. In multicultural schools, language skills are among the main factors defining learning trajectories from basic education to upper-secondary education and beyond among young people with immigrant backgrounds. Ensuring adequate Finnish language skills provides better educational opportunities for all students. However, supporting learning in Finnish is an issue that requires ethical sensitivity from the school community in communicating to families the importance of language learning for future educational opportunities.

The third category of challenges related to school leadership concerned the principals' own professional development. For example, the challenge for the male Finnish principal quoted below, who had worked 11 years in a school with approximately 1000 students in a multicultural and low socio-economical area, was his own wellbeing. He described his situation in the following way:

> I am devoted to my school, but, at the same time, I feel that I am close to burnout, and I need to take a break from this work. I am doing everything as well as I can, but I plan to take a leave of absence to learn how to build wooden boats. When I retire, I will spend time with my boat, and I'll do some sailing. (Jaakko, Helsinki, Finland, Tirri et al., 2021, p. 8)

Burnout is a serious problem that commonly afflicts those working as teachers and in helping and serving professions (Pyhältö et al., 2021; Salmela-Aro et al., 2019). This principal demonstrates responsibility, courage and honesty in acknowledging his own limitations. In our study with exemplar principals, the moral virtues of wisdom and knowledge, humanity, courage, justice, transcendence and temperance have been identified as important in creating ethical leadership (Eisenschmidt et al., 2019). Moreover, according to the Finnish ethical code for teachers, it is important for teachers to take care of their own wellbeing in order to be able to help their students.

4   Questions to Reflect on by Yourself or with Your Peers

– What does ethical sensitivity mean in a teacher's work? In what kinds of situations is it required?
– What kinds of challenges do students and their families from other countries and cultures present for a teacher's work?
– Become familiar with the items measuring ethical sensitivity in Table 2 and ponder how well these items describe ethical sensitivity in the context of teaching, studying, and learning. You can also evaluate your own level of ethical sensitivity.
– Become familiar with Figure 3 and consider the cultural dependency of ethical sensitivity. How do Finland, Estonia and Iran differ in ethical sensitivity and what could explain these differences?
– Ponder how schools could enhance a sense of communality between students, teachers and parents with different cultural backgrounds.

– What are the current ethical challenges in schools? Reflect on and compare the challenges presented in this chapter to the ones in the schools
of your country.
– What kind of moral conflicts can teachers experience in their work? How
can ethical sensitivity help teachers find constructive solutions?
– Reflect on unfair situations in your own life related to schooling? What
was the situation? Who treated you unfairly? How did the situation
end? Is there something you or the people involved could have done
differently?
– What kind of ethical sensitivity is required from a teacher in collaboration with homes?

The Purposeful Teacher

The previous chapters emphasized that teaching involves multiple moral dilemmas, conflicts, and challenges. The development of ethical expertise in teaching is demanding and time consuming. Teachers require long-term goals and resilience to continue in their profession. Similarly, students require long-term goals to develop the stamina and motivation to continue in their studies. In this chapter, we present the purposeful teacher as a goal for teacher education and an important part of professional ethics. Purposeful teachers are educators who have found their own purpose in teaching and use content knowledge and pedagogical content knowledge for developing purpose in their students.

1 Purpose in Teacher's Professional Ethics

One of the most important goals of human existence is to find a clear purpose and place in life. Ideally, one's chosen occupation and work can provide such a purpose. The teaching profession has often been regarded as a calling (Hansen, 1995; Tirri et al., 1999). The teacher's task is to help students develop holistically. In turn, students' task is to view studying as meaningful and reflect on the purpose of their lives. Reflection with students on a purpose in life is one of the tasks of a holistic educator in all subjects and grade levels. Moreover, teachers cannot explain the purpose of studying different subjects without first reflecting on a purpose in life. The following questions are particularly challenging for teachers in their work:
- Why is it important to study different subjects, for example, mathematics or religion?
- What is the long-term purpose of education?
- How does the subject students are studying relate to their current life situation?

William Damon is one of the best-known researchers in topics related to a purpose in life. His perspective is developmental and holistic and excellently suited to education and teacher education contexts. Damon defines a purpose in life in the following way:

> Purpose is a stable and generalized intention to accomplish something that is at once meaningful to the self and of consequence to the world beyond the self. (Damon et al., 2003, p. 121)

Damon's definition was influenced by the thinking of the founder of logope-dics, Victor Frankl's (1905–1997), on responsibility and 'giving to the world' and the view that a purpose in life is nonreligious by nature (Frankl, 1988). It does not require belief in God or commitment to any worldview. On the other hand, his definition allows for the inclusion of these aspects in one's purpose in life. Typically, according to Damon's definition:

1. A purpose in life is meaningful to the self. It is something that inspires and motivates a person and is personally important. A purpose in life is a con-crete goal that can be reached in the long-term. This is how a purpose in life differs from the general and philosophical concept of the meaning of life.
2. A purpose in life is not only a dream or fantasy, as an individual is commit-ted to realizing it and makes plans and choices and acts in order to attain it.
3. A purpose in life also benefits others and not only the self. (This moral prosocial emphasis distinguishes Damon's definition from many other definitions.)

Based on Damon's definition, earning money to become wealthy does not fulfil the criteria for a purpose in life. On the other hand, purposes that include the goals of helping others and building society do fulfil these criteria. Both the Finnish ethical code for teachers and the National Core Curriculum for Basic Education emphasize this beyond-the-self dimension. For teachers, this means acting in the best interest of students and working with students to support their growth into moral citizens.

2   Teachers' Purposes

2.1   *Teachers' Purpose Profiles*
Based on empirical studies, William Damon identifies four different groups into which young people can be categorized based on their purpose in life. He terms these groups disengaged, dreamers, dabblers and purposeful (Damon, 2008, p. 59). The same categorization can be applied to teachers.

From a teaching perspective, the *disengaged* are teachers who neither can formulate goals for their teaching nor are even interested in searching for such goals. Some disengaged teachers are not committed to anything, while oth-ers pursue hedonistic goals or self-promotion. *Dreamers* fantasize about goals they do not currently pursue, such as hypothetical educational ideals. They have taken no action to realize these ideals. Thus, they have idealistic dreams related to teaching and learning but lack concrete plans and practices.

Dabblers are teachers who might appear purposeful. For example, they may have participated in in-service education for teachers, but these experiences have failed to produce either concrete action in their teaching or plans with a long-term perspective. Such teachers change their teaching methods or educational philosophies without reflecting on the goals they wish to achieve in their teaching. Their interests are too short and transient to develop into goals they can commit to.

By contrast, *purposeful* teachers 'are ethical professionals with long-term commitment to their students and educational goals they intend to meet in their teaching' (Tirri, 2018, p. 222). They can justify the goals they wish to achieve in their teaching and have found a purpose that inspires them in their everyday work and helps them to see the meaning of their work for the future. These teachers have taken concrete action to realize their goals and promote their educational philosophy.

Table 7 presents the purpose profiles of Finnish teachers by adapting Damon's model (Tirri & Kuusisto, 2016a). The profiles can provide help in planning teachers' professional development both in preservice and in-service teacher education. The direction of development is from a disengaged to a purposeful teacher. The profiles can be used to search for the general purpose of teaching and in reflection on the specific purposes of different subjects.

2.2   *Contents of Teachers' Purposes*

We discuss next the kinds of purposes Finnish pre- and in-service teachers identify for themselves. The participants in our study were Finnish preservice teachers (n = 912) and practicing teachers (n = 77) who were asked to describe

TABLE 7   Teachers' purpose profiles

Purpose profile	Description
Disengaged	Disengaged teachers express no purposes for their teaching and are uninterested in searching for them.
Dreamers	Dreamers possess ideals about teaching and learning but do not actualize them.
Dabblers	Dabblers participate in in-service education for teachers, but they fail to internalize these experiences or reflect on and apply them professionally.
Purposeful	Purposeful teachers have identified the purpose of their teaching and are committed to it with long-term goals. They possess a clear understanding of what they wish to achieve and the justification for these goals.

TABLE 8 Finnish pre- and in-service teachers' purposes according to their written statements (from Kuusisto & Tirri, 2021, p. 5)

Categories in the statements	Preservice teachers ($N = 912$)						In-service teachers ($N = 77$)					
			Self		Other				Self		Other	
	N	%	n	%	n	%	N	%	n	%	n	%
Happiness	568	62	520	57	182	20	55	71	52	68	20	26
Relationships	402	44	318	35	133	15	10	13	5	6	5	6
Work	311	34	274	30	69	8	11	14	8	10	3	4
Self-actualization	245	27	240	26	23	3	21	27	21	27		
Hedonism	158	17	158	17	3	0	11	14	11	14		
Social issues	112	12	26	3	96	11	3	4			3	4
Political influence	105	12	19	2	94	10	5	6	1	1	4	5
Economic goals	70	8	69	8	5	1	1	1	1	1		
Religion	51	6	37	4	24	3						
Health	44	5	43	5	5	1	4	5	4	5		
Aesthetics	29	3	24	3	8	1	1	1	1	1		

in *their own words* their purpose in life and how they incorporate aspects of their professional life into this purpose (Kuusisto & Tirri, 2021).

Table 8 presents Finnish teachers' written statements on their purpose in life. Happiness was identified as the most frequently mentioned aim. Over half of preservice teachers (62%) and in-service teachers (71%) wished to pursue a good and happy life. Happiness was the ultimate goal, meaning the participants sought to realize it through other purposes, such as self-actualization or having a family. On the other hand, happiness was understood as a prerequisite for realizing other, more important purposes, as this teacher wrote:

> When I am happy, I am a better mum. (Preservice teacher 2271, Kuusisto & Tirri, 2021, p. 6)

Other popular purposes concerned relationships (44%), work (34%), and self-actualization (27%). Teachers aimed to have their own family, raise children and cherish close friendships.

Preservice teachers, in particular, wished to find meaningful work. The teachers used words like 'work,' 'job,' and 'occupation,' which in the context of teacher education could refer to the teaching profession. Nevertheless, some preservice teachers seemed to mean other occupations, and some wrote about their uncertainty with regard to their professional choice:

> Professionally, I do not have a clear purpose, even though I am studying to become a teacher. (Preservice teacher 4129, Kuusisto & Tirri, 2021, p. 8)

For 10% (*n* = 100) of preservice teachers, teaching was explicitly mentioned as their dream, calling or purpose. The following quotations reflect the ideals of a purposeful teacher:

> My purpose in life is to teach what I can and whom I can, to help others grow and understand life. (Preservice teacher 1064, Kuusisto & Tirri, 2021, p. 8)

> [For me the most important purpose is to have a happy relationship and family life] and secondly to defend children's rights to a good life and participate in their upbringing as a Kindergarten teacher. (Preservice teacher 1330, Kuusisto & Tirri, 2021, p. 8)

Teachers also wanted to learn new things, develop themselves, live in accordance with their own values and help others to do the same, as this preservice teacher wrote:

> My purpose is to be my authentic self and also to help other people to be what they truly are. (Preservice teacher 1378, Kuusisto & Tirri, 2021, p. 6)

Purposes that were mentioned by under 20% of the teachers were related to hedonism (enjoying life, having fun), social issues (helping others, voluntary work), political influence (helping at a societal and global level), economic goals (having enough money, owning a home), religion, health, and aesthetics (making music or writing books).

All of the content categories were found to reflect both a self-orientation (the teacher wanted to be happy) and a beyond-the-self orientation (the teacher wished to advance the happiness of other people and especially the happiness of their own family and friends). However, the majority of purposes were clearly self-oriented (Table 8). Only when teachers were writing about purposes related to social issues (helping others) and political influence were they inclined to contribute to the wellbeing of others more than their own.

Figure 4 summarizes teachers' purpose orientations. The majority of teachers had identified at least one content category, thus these Finnish teachers

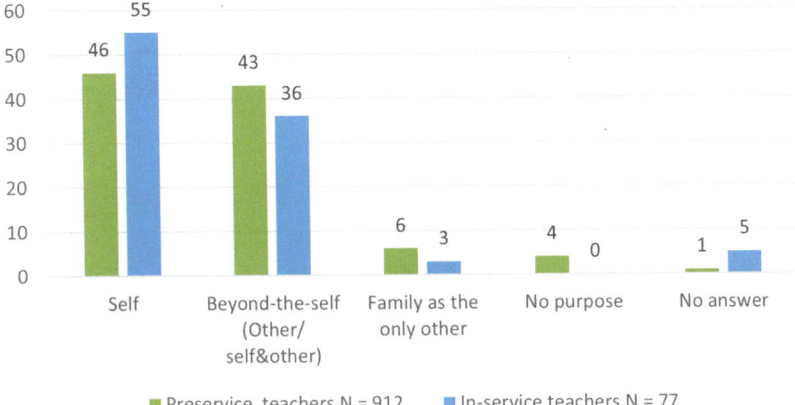

FIGURE 4   Self- and beyond-the-self orientations among Finnish teachers (Note: the numbers above the bars denote percentages)

had found meaningful goals for their lives. However, nearly half (preservice teachers 46%, in-service teachers 55%) showed only a self-orientation. By contrast, approximately 40% of the teachers (pre-service teachers 43%, in-service teachers 36%) displayed a beyond-the-self orientation, implying a purpose and a profile of a purposeful teacher.

For a few teachers, taking care of their own family and children was the only aspect of their orientation to benefit others. Moreover, some teachers mentioned that they lacked a purpose in life or wrote that these types of questions should not be discussed at all. In addition, a small number failed to answer.

To investigate further teachers' associations between their purpose and teaching, we asked in-service teachers (N = 77) to write their views on the topic. As Table 9 illustrates, when explicitly addressing this question, 78% of teachers saw teaching as a medium or instrument for realizing their purpose in life. This time, a beyond-the-self -orientation was more strongly present in teachers' answers (44%). Nevertheless, one third of teachers (33%) viewed teaching as beneficial for their individual life goals. For a few teachers, purpose and teaching were unconnected.

Teachers also require goals that extend beyond the self in their work. If teaching is seen as a purpose in life instead of a job, the work becomes meaningful and teachers also wish to help their students find a purpose in their own lives. Researchers in teacher education frequently discuss the notion of vision, which provides motivation and helps teachers reflect on their work (Husu & Tirri, 2007; Tirri & Husu, 2006). Teachers' trust in their ability to positively influence their students' lives helps them commit to their work. In schools, teachers should be able to teach in such a way that students consider the

TABLE 9   Teachers' perceptions on how teaching manifests in their life purposes
(from Kuusisto & Tirri, 2021, p. 8)

Categories	In-service teachers	
	$N = 77$	%
Teaching as a medium for realizing purpose	60	78
Beyond-the-self orientation (Other or self and other)	34	44
Self-orientation	26	33
No role	5	6.5
Unclear answer	12	15.5

subject to be personally significant and studying to be a meaningful activity
(Darling-Hammond, 1990).

3   Purposeful Teaching

Purposeful teaching supports the goals of school education. It refers to holistic
education that aims to place the subject taught in a meaningful framework and
demonstrate its relevance to students' personal development. For example,
in 2014 the goals of basic education in the Finnish National Core Curriculum
were updated to include students' reflections on the connections between the
past, the present and the future and the meanings of their own choices, lifestyles, and actions to themselves and their communities, society and nature.
At the same time, the curriculum requires students to acquire skills to evaluate the actions of their communities and society and to advance sustainable
development (FNBE, 2016).

The current curriculum thus topicalizes reflection on a purpose in life.
Teaching about a purpose in life supports reflection on the choices and actions
in one's own life not only within the framework of the self but also from the
perspective of the community, society and nature. The Finnish curriculum
guides students to commit themselves to pro-active actions to build a sustainable future. The curriculum goals emphasize finding a clear purpose in life that
students are committed to realizing and that is meaningful both to themselves
and others (Damon et al., 2003).

According to Damon (2008), the task of an educator is to help young people
identify a sustainable and long-term purpose for their lives that supports their
development and holistic growth. He suggests that the problems of young

people are often unrelated to overly demanding requirements and ambitious goals; instead, they are due to excessively low goals and a lack of purpose in life (Damon, 1995). This lack of purpose causes addictions, depression, antisocial behavior and indolence in students. By contrast, finding a purpose in life supports prosocial behavior, moral commitment, achievement and high self-esteem (Damon, 2008). In order to find a purpose in life, young people require help from educators. In a comparative study among Finnish and American young people, participants were asked what kind of help they required in their search for purpose. According to the findings, both American and Finnish students (13–19-year-olds) required teachers' support in finding a purpose for their studies and lives (Bundick & Tirri, 2014).

In discussions on a purpose in life, the teacher serves as an example and role-model of an adult who can identify and verbalize important issues in life (Malin et al., 2013, p. 195). Research has demonstrated that such reflections on a purpose in life positively influence students' goal-orientation and satisfaction (Bundick, 2011). Moreover, searching for a vision and planning for the future together with a teacher advances students' ability to set goals and commit to achieving them in a purposeful and systematic manner (Bundick & Tirri, 2014; Nurmi, 1991).

3.1   Interactive Relationships in Teaching

The German concept *Bildung* refers to holistic education and teaching. It includes development as an individual and a member of a society. Teaching is realized through interaction between the teacher, student(s) and the study material (Herbart, 1835). The teaching-studying-learning process (Kansanen et al., 2000) includes important interactive relationships that are depicted in the didactical triangle in Figure 5. A teacher's relationship with a student is termed a *pedagogical relationship* (Stadius, 1967, p. 25). The teacher and student are equal as human beings, but the teacher holds a professional role that conveys power and responsibility in the relationship with the student. This causes the pedagogical relationship to be asymmetric in nature (Kansanen & Meri, 1991). The pedagogical relationship also includes a pedagogical paradox: the teacher's goal is to help students become so independent that the teacher is no longer required (Kant, 2007). Teachers master the content of their teaching, and the goal of teaching is to create similar relationship between the student and the subject that is studied. However, even though teachers possess knowledge of their own subject and are passionate about it, they also require *pedagogical content knowledge* to be able to teach the subject in such a way that their students learn (Shulman, 1986, 1987). Pedagogical content knowledge distinguishes the teacher from other experts in the field, who master the content but lack pedagogical knowledge. The *didactical relationship* refers to teachers' relationship with their students' studying and learning (Kansanen & Meri, 1999).

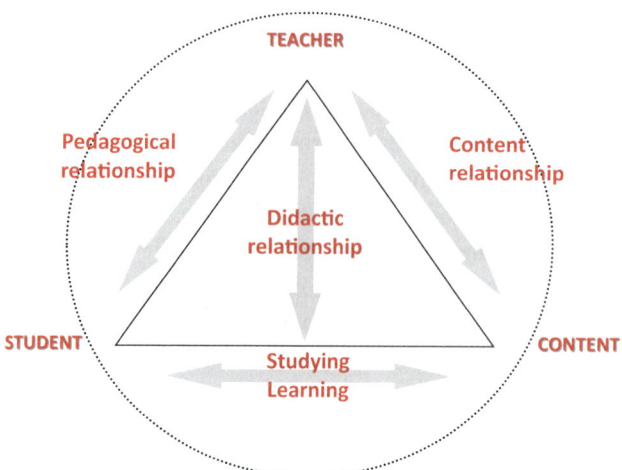

FIGURE 5   Didactic triangle (see Herbart, 1835; Kansanen & Meri, 1999; Tirri & Kuusisto, 2016b; Toom, 2006)

With the aid of the didactical relationship, the teacher helps the student create a personal relationship with the content. Teachers enjoy the pedagogical and didactical freedom to use any method they wish that adheres to the goals in the curriculum in order to open the meaning of the content to their students.

In teaching based on German didactics, the content may contain many meanings. However, 'there is no content without meaning and no meaning without content' (Hopmann, 2007, p. 116). Meaning is created through a teacher's methodological decisions, for example by explaining and justifying to students why the content and course materials are important or by students' written reflection on the meaningfulness of the subject (Durik & Harackiewicz, 2007; Hulleman & Harackiewicz, 2009). In a study published in the journal Science, Chris Hulleman and Judith Harackiewicz demonstrated that, for academically weak students, personal reflection on the subject matter studied in science had a statistically significant effect on success in their studies. However, this intervention had no influence on the success of high-achieving students (Hulleman & Harackiewicz, 2009).

3.2   *General and Subject Specific Purposes in Teaching*

In two Finnish studies, teachers and preservice teachers were asked to identify the most important purposes in their teaching (Tirri, 2012; Tirri & Ubani, 2013). The teachers' answers contained general purposes that were common to all teachers in the study. Both practicing teachers and preservice teachers, irrespective of their subject, viewed themselves as responsible professionals whose task it was to teach the basic elements of their subjects. Moreover, they described themselves as holistic educators who were responsible for the development of their students' personalities and ethics. Teaching experience was visible in their answers such that experienced teachers were more likely than preservice teachers to emphasize the needs of their students. By contrast, preservice teachers paid more attention to their skills and knowledge. This variation can be explained by the different developmental stages of the teachers surveyed. Novice teachers are uncertain and concentrate on developing their own skills. The greater experience of expert teachers, on the other hand, allows them to concentrate more on their students (Berliner, 1991; Huberman, 1992).

In this research, subject-specific purposes were also evident. The most statistically significant differences were found between teachers of mathematics and teachers of religious education (Tirri, 2012; Tirri & Ubani, 2013). According to the results, both practicing and preservice mathematics teachers emphasized the need to acknowledge different learners in their teaching, for example gifted students and girls. Mathematics is often seen as a male subject, and girls can thus underestimate their skills (Cvencek et al., 2011). The teachers in the study were aware of this tendency and thus consciously encouraged girls to study mathematics. Moreover, mathematics is often seen as a difficult subject, and teachers wished to identify potential giftedness and support it in their teaching.

By contrast, both in-service and preservice religious education teachers emphasized the importance of personal reflection regarding the subject taught. This emphasis is also easy to understand, as in Finland religious education has always been a subject about which people have strong preconceptions. Ethically sensitive teachers can acknowledge timely ethical issues related to the subject and teach them to their students in ways that help them form their own opinions.

3.3   Cultural Differences in Purposeful Teaching

In the same way as teaching any subject or topic, to become a purposeful teacher requires acquisition of and reflection on *content knowledge* about a purpose in life in general. For example, teachers could ask themselves the following questions:
- Why is purpose important for holistic wellbeing and learning? Why is it essential that a purpose in life includes a long-term commitment to its realization and a beyond-the-self orientation?
- How does purpose develop? What are purpose profiles? What kind of purposes do young people typically have?
- What is my own purpose in life? What kind of purpose profile do I have at the moment? How are my purposes in life and my profession linked?

By answering these questions, teachers build their *content relationship*, which in turn is important for guiding students towards finding their own purposes.

In purposeful teaching, teachers also require *pedagogical content knowledge*, meaning that teaching takes accounts of students' age, learning styles, and current developmental level to ensure that it supports individual and process-focused learning. In one of our studies, we examined teachers' self-evaluations of their pedagogical approaches to teaching purpose and supporting students' purpose development (Kuusisto et al., 2016). We investigated whether teachers explicitly discussed purpose in the classroom or implicitly taught it through revealing the personal relevance of the subject being taught. In this study, the participants were in-service teachers from Finland (n = 464) and Iran (n = 556).

Figure 6 shows the results and how Iranian teachers advocated an explicit style in which a purpose in life was discussed openly with students, while Finnish teachers utilized more implicit styles by showing the relevance of the subjects they taught. The Iranian findings can be explained by the aims of the Iranian curriculum and educational system, where, after the 1979 Islamic revolution, the government has required that every teacher from elementary school to higher education advances students' commitment to the Iranian interpretation of the Islamic faith and values (Hedayati et al., 2017b). In other words, Iranian society has a clear idea of the kind of purpose that should be internalized. Finnish teachers instead, emphasized teaching the personal meaningfulness of the subject, which in turn reflects the Finnish tradition of didactics, indicating that the teacher facilitates the learning process by creating a personal relationship between the students and the subject they study regardless of the topic or subject in question.

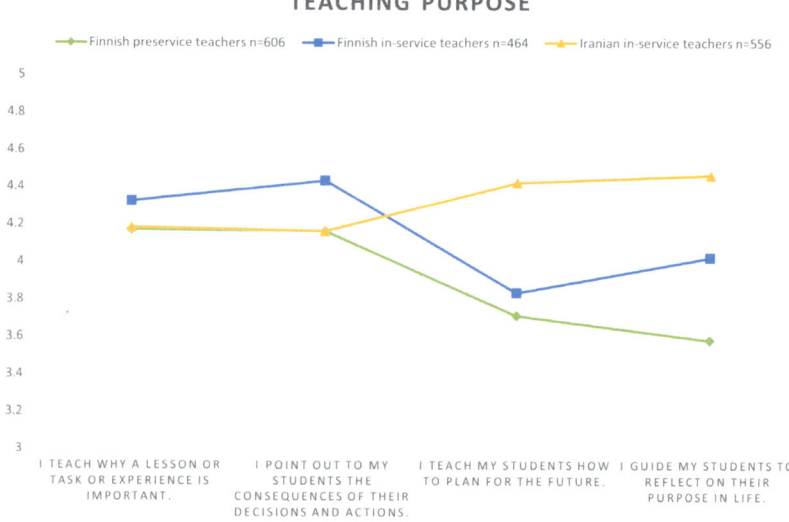

FIGURE 6   Teaching purpose evaluated by Finnish and Iranian teachers

We also found that Finnish subject teachers of mathematics and science experienced greater challenges in teaching purpose than other teachers. By contrast, religious education teachers found instruction on purpose the most natural, which is unsurprising since this subject involves discussion of life's 'big questions' in order to build student's worldviews (Kuusisto et al., 2016). Nevertheless, the results raise questions for teacher education, particularly concerning mathematics and science teachers. Teacher education should equip such teachers with pedagogical ideas that help students recognize the personal relevance of these subjects and realize how they can be used to contribute to society and help others (Hulleman & Harakiewicz, 2009; Yeager et al., 2014).

Figure 6 shows that the scores for Finnish in-service and preservice teachers were similar: both highlighted teaching personal relevance more than explicit discussions about purpose.

The preservice teachers who self-evaluated how they would teach purpose also provided answers related to the dimensions and content of purpose. Thus, we were able to analyze how purposeful teaching was predicted by such dimensions (*purpose found* [Steger et al., 2006], *engagement* [Ryff, 1989; Ryff & Keys, 1995], *helping* [Roberts & Robins, 2000], *content* – relationships, hedonistic, economic, political influence, religion and aesthetics – [Roberts & Robins, 2000] and the *search for purpose* [Steger et al., 2006]). The results showed that a *purpose found*, the *search for purpose* and *helping* predicted purposeful teaching (Tirri & Kuusisto, 2019). Instead, purposeful teaching was not predicted by either engagement in realizing one's own purpose or any of the content categories. This could be explained by the teachers' written answers, which demonstrated that their personal purpose was mostly related to pursuing happiness and close relationships. The results presented in this chapter show a surprisingly strong self-orientation among Finnish teachers, which presents challenges for teacher education and the educational system.

3.4   *Didactic Model of Purposeful Teaching in Teacher Education*
Figure 7 presents a didactical model of purposeful teaching in teacher education based on German didactics (Hopmann, 2007; Toom et al., 2015). In the first phase of the process, preservice teachers write a description of a purposeful teaching or learning event during their own schooling. The goal of this phase is to identify the personal experiences of preservice teachers and guide them to reflect on these experiences. The preservice teachers are asked to write from their own experiences with the help of concrete questions that assist them in their reflection and writing. In this phase, it is important to relive the purposeful event and attempt to remember the details and feelings associated with it.

At the second stage, preservice teachers are divided into small groups in which they are told to reflect on their purposeful experiences in more

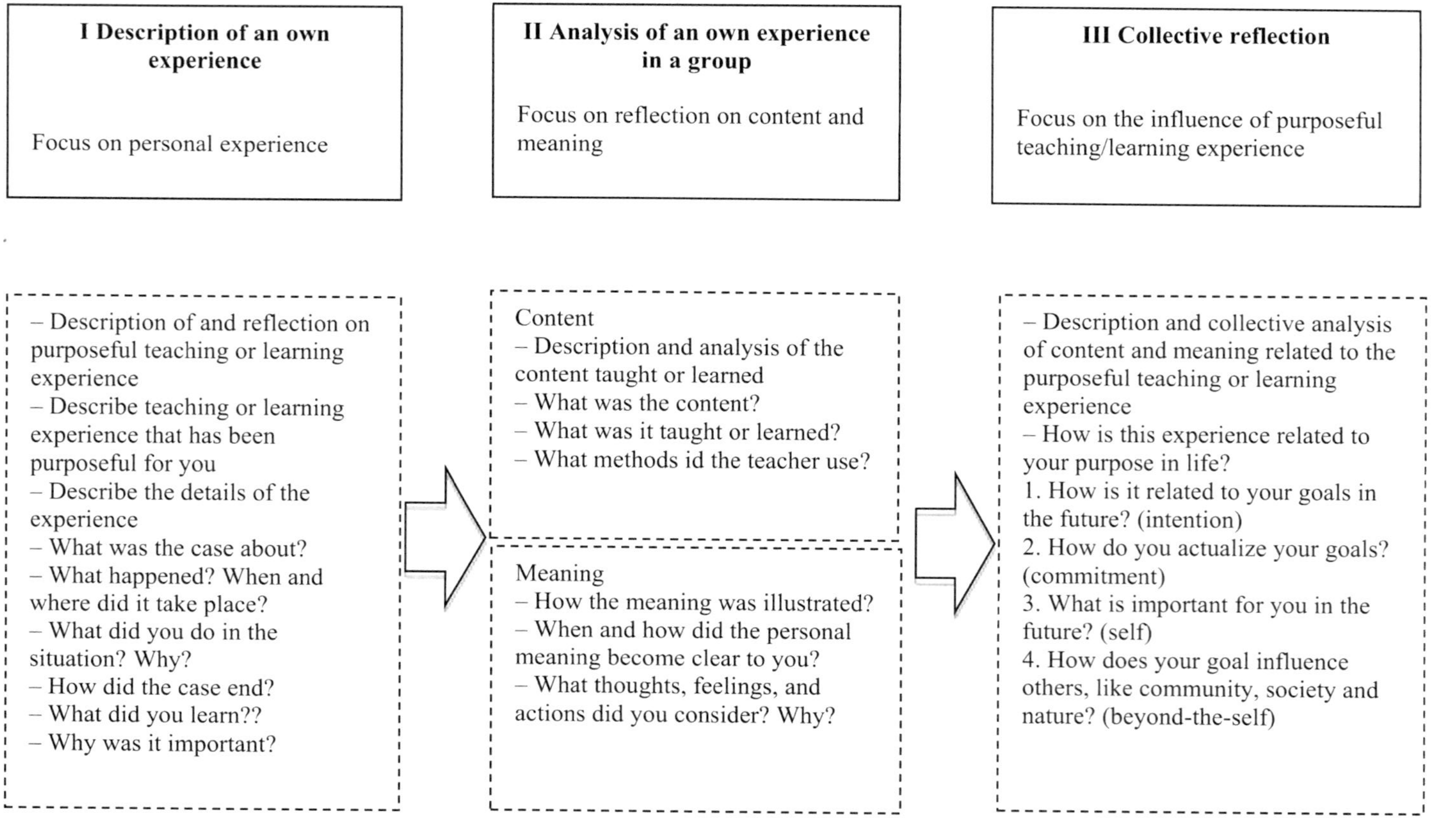

I Description of an own experience

Focus on personal experience

II Analysis of an own experience in a group

Focus on reflection on content and meaning

III Collective reflection

Focus on the influence of purposeful teaching/learning experience

– Description of and reflection on purposeful teaching or learning experience
– Describe teaching or learning experience that has been purposeful for you
– Describe the details of the experience
– What was the case about?
– What happened? When and where did it take place?
– What did you do in the situation? Why?
– How did the case end?
– What did you learn??
– Why was it important?

Content
– Description and analysis of the content taught or learned
– What was the content?
– What was it taught or learned?
– What methods id the teacher use?

Meaning
– How the meaning was illustrated?
– When and how did the personal meaning become clear to you?
– What thoughts, feelings, and actions did you consider? Why?

– Description and collective analysis of content and meaning related to the purposeful teaching or learning experience
– How is this experience related to your purpose in life?
1. How is it related to your goals in the future? (intention)
2. How do you actualize your goals? (commitment)
3. What is important for you in the future? (self)
4. How does your goal influence others, like community, society and nature? (beyond-the-self)

FIGURE 7   A didactical model of purposeful teaching in teacher education (adapted from Toom et al., 2015; Tirri & Kuusisto, 2016b)

systematic ways. Now the purpose is to guide preservice teachers to reflect on the contents and meanings of the experience (Hopmann, 2007). What was the issue taught or learnt in the experience? How was the meaning of the issue opened up? Here, preservice teachers analyze their experiences and reflect on the contexts of the situation, routines, habits, and human relationships with the help of the questions provided.

In the third phase, preservice teachers jointly discuss their experiences and their different perspectives on them. The goal is to create new understandings of the situations in cooperation with a teacher and peers. Collective reflection allows a better and deeper understanding of the essential factors of these situations. In such discussions, a more general picture of the spectrum of purposeful experiences is formed that lays the foundation for finding purpose in teaching and learning. Finally, preservice teachers are asked to write a reflective essay on the second and third phases of the process. A teacher can use the stages in Bloom's taxonomy in the evaluation of these essays (see Chapter 6 and Figure 11).

4   Students' Purposes

In order to help students in their reflections on and search for a purpose in life, it is important for teachers to understanding the individual circumstances of their students. In the same way as a teacher evaluates students' learning in different subjects, holistic growth and the development of purpose are to be acknowledged, diagnosed, and acted upon in school. Some students require support in their overall sense of purpose, some in pursuing that purpose and some in broadening their concerns beyond the self. Teachers must also recognize those students who thrive and possess clear visions as they enjoy addressing the multiple opportunities and new openings available to them (Damon, 2008). To offer some concrete examples for teachers, in this section we present the purposes in life identified by secondary school students in different countries. In our research, the participating students (n = 386) were 13–18-year-olds from different parts of Finland. We compare their purposes with those of US (n = 1250) and Brazilian (n = 275) young people (see Damon et al., 2009; Tirri & Kuusisto, 2019).

4.1   *Students' Purpose Profiles*
Finnish students' purpose profiles were created based on three dimensions of Damon et al.'s definition of purpose (Damon et al., 2003): the extent to which students feel that they have *found* a purpose (Steger et al., 2006), their level of

commitment to *actualizing* this purpose (Ryff, 1989; Ryff & Keys, 1995), and the importance of *helping and contributing to others* in that purpose (Roberts & Robins, 2000).

The profiles were named in line with the categories defined in Seana Moran's study, presented below in Table 10 (Moran, 2009, p. 147). While Moran uses the same three proposed by Damon – *disengaged, dreamers*, and *purposeful* (Damon, 2008) she also includes a group termed *self-oriented* youth, which refers to young people who have identified and committed to realizing important goals but lack the motivation to help others and contribute beyond the self.

Figure 8, in turn, depicts the four purpose profiles we identified among Finnish students (Tirri & Kuusisto, 2019). All profiles differed statistically

TABLE 10   Purpose profiles in relation to actualization and beyond-the-self
            aspects of purpose (from Moran 2009, p. 147)

	High	Dreamer	Purposeful
Beyond-the-self			
	Low	Disengaged	Self-oriented
		Low High
		Actualization

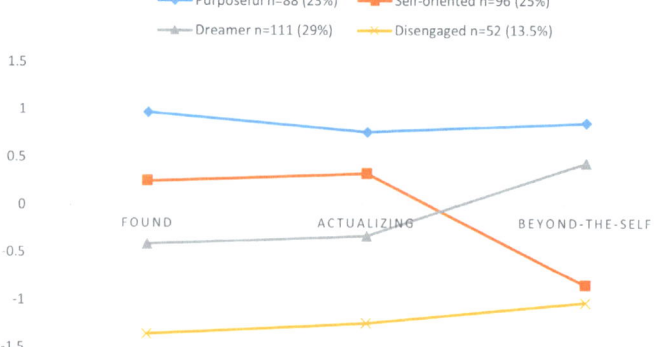

FIGURE 8   Purpose profiles of Finnish students (means are standardized z-values, since two
            instruments contained a scale of 1–7 and one 1–5)

significantly from each other in all dimensions apart from helping in the case of disengaged and self-oriented students, which was equally unimportant for either profile.

The largest group, accounting for almost one third of students, was dreamers (n = 111, 29%). These students had not yet fully found their purpose and thus were not actively working to realize it. However, helping others was important to them. Nevertheless, for dreamers, purpose was gradually taking shape. From an educator's perspective, these students could benefit from teacher help in identifying concrete ways to participate and contribute, such as encouraging them to take on small-scale responsibilities and participate, for example, in voluntary work. When dreamers gradually begin to realize their visions to help others, their sense of purpose and agency becomes stronger (Damon, 2008).

In turn, one fourth of students were *self-oriented* (n = 96, 25%). They had found meaningful aims and were engaged in realizing them, but they were uninterested in benefiting others. Since this profile lacks a beyond-the-self dimension, within Damon et al.'s framework these students are not yet considered to possess a purpose. Instead, they have *life goals* that they pursue. From the teacher's perspective, these students require help in learning to recognize the needs of others and shape their life goals in a prosocial direction, in line with the goals of the National Core Curriculum (see FNBE, 2016). Self-orientation seems to be growing trend in many cultures (Moran, 2019). For instance, even in countries that have traditionally valued communality, such as Iran and China, today young people emphasize materialistic and self-oriented life goals (Hedayati et al., 2017c; Jiang & Gao, 2018).

Almost one fourth of students were *purposeful* (n = 88, 23%). These students had found a purpose, were engaged in realizing it, and wanted to help others. From the teacher's perspective, it should be noted that even purposeful students require teacher support in developing and deepening their purpose. Purpose development is a process where purpose is revised throughout the life course (Bronk, 2014).

Over 10% of students were identified as *disengaged* (n = 52, 13.5%). They had not found their purpose, were not pursuing it, and were uninterested in helping others. This group seems to be in potential danger of dropping out, sliding outside education and working life and becoming so called NEETs, in other words young people who are *not in education, employment or training* (Damon, 2008). In schools, it is crucial that teachers are able to recognize these students and offer help to allow them to identify a meaningful purpose for their lives.

The proportion of students belonging to the profiles identified in Finland was somewhat similar to that in Moran's research, in which the participants were 12–22-year-old (N = 270) young people from the US (Moran, 2009). For example, parallel to our study, Moran found that one fourth of young Americans were self-oriented (25%) or purposeful (25%). However, in the US young people were found to be disengaged (40%), while the smallest group was dreamers (10%). Moran also acknowledged that among college students the number of disengaged students was smaller. Having a place to study and prospects for a future career seemed to increase both purposefulness and self-orientation among US youth. Therefore, for example, the extension of compulsory education in Finland from 16 to 18 years of age in 2020 (Finlex, 2020) appears to be a promising attempt to support students' holistic growth.

Purpose profiles are useful tools for teachers in identifying and diagnosing their students' purpose development. However, in addition to the profiles themselves, teachers need to know their content. This informs teachers about students' interests and helps them create a relationship with students' learning, i.e., a didactical relationship. The nature of students' purposes also reveals how a beyond-the-self orientation, which is a crucial element in Damon's purpose definition, is manifested in their thinking and behavior.

4.2   *Contents of Student Purposes in Three Countries*

Next, the contents of purposes held by Finnish (n = 386), the US (n = 1247) and Brazilian (n = 260) students (Damon et al., 2009; Tirri & Kuusisto, 2019) are examined. The students were asked to choose the most important purpose from the list presented in Figure 9. Students were also advised to ponder each item on a scale of 1–7 (1 = strongly disagree, 7 = strongly agree) and answer the question 'How much do you agree or disagree with the following statements? The purpose of my life is to ...' (for more about the instrument, see Bundick et al., 2006).

Finnish students' purpose in life most often concerned family and friends (25%) and having fun (16%). By contrast, those in the US selected serving God or a higher power (16%) and family and friends (14%). In turn, the rankings of their Brazilian counterparts were more evenly distributed between family and friends (13%), a good career (12%), making the world a better place (12%) and earning other people's respect (12%).

In all three countries, family and friends made life purposeful for young people. When measured on a scale of 1–7, religion was among the least pursued purposes and contained the largest standard deviation, also in the US, which means that for some, youth spirituality seemed to provide the basis for their life and purpose, while for others it was not meaningful at all.

Within Damon's framework, we were naturally interested in whether the aims of the participants were self-serving, indicating a self orientation (life goal),

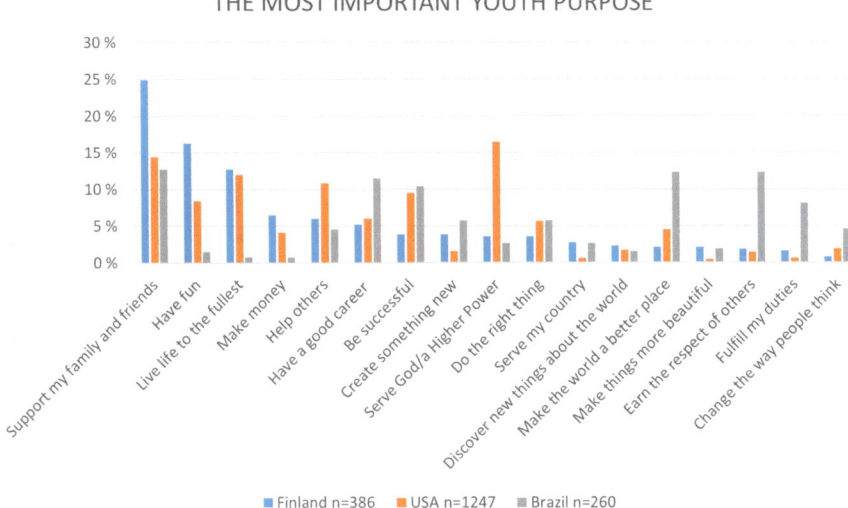

FIGURE 9   The most important purpose among Finnish, US and Brazilian young people

or associated with serving others, indicating a beyond-the-self orientation (purpose). The orientation of the student is not always clear judged by the items alone. For example, supporting family and friends could be associated with self-centeredness or contributing to a better world. Thus, we used a principal component analysis of the 17 items to examine whether family was understood as part of the self or whether supporting the family was an indicator of a beyond-the-self orientation with (Figure 9). In all three countries, the items loaded on two components: advancing one's own life (self-orientation) and making the world a better place (beyond-the-self-orientation) (Tirri & Kuusisto, 2019).

Among Finnish youth, family and friends were part of advancing their own life and were associated with the same category as career, money, success, duties, having fun, gaining other people's respect and doing things right. Instead, the US and Brazilian young people linked family and friends with making the world a better place. In America, family, religion and country were associated with helping others. Similarly, in Brazil, making the world a better place was linked with home and religion (Brazilian young people did not evaluate the item 'serving your country'). Among US and Brazilian youth, success in their own life was related to economic achievements, career, and fun. Nevertheless, in all three countries, they emphasized their *own lives* more than their contribution to the world (Figure 10). These results indicate that teachers should specifically focus on helping students broaden their interests to find a purpose in serving and benefiting others.

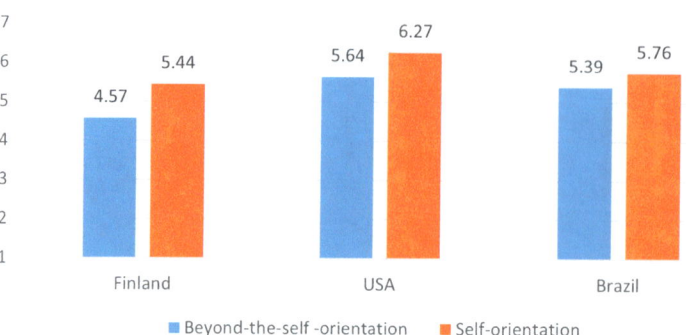

FIGURE 10   Means of purpose orientations among Finnish, US, and Brazilian youth

5   Questions to Reflect on by Yourself or with Your Peers

– What is your purpose in life? Compare your answers with your peers.
– Evaluate William Damon's definition of a purpose in life. Do you agree with it or do you want to present your own definition?
– Reflect on the nature of the pedagogical relationship and your own role in it. What are your challenges as a teacher?
– What is your relationship with the content you teach? Do you master all the content you teach equally? Do you have a favorite subject? Do you find any subject or theme unpleasant or challenging? Reflect on how you could improve your relationship with the content in those subjects that are difficult for you.
– What does pedagogical content knowledge mean? How does it differ from simple content knowledge?
– What is the didactical relationship? How could you improve the didactical relationship in ways that would increase your students' motivation to study?
– What methods can you use to open the meaning of the subject you teach to your students? Exchange ideas in a group.
– What purposes guide your teaching? How are they related to the purposes in your own life and the purposes presented in the curriculum?
– Discuss the different purpose profiles in Table 7. In what group do you belong? Why?

- Both practicing teachers and preservice teachers evaluated happiness as their most important purpose in life. Ponder the content of happiness. What makes you happy as a person and as a teacher?
- Become familiar with the teachers' written answers on purpose presented in this chapter. What is your purpose personally and professionally? Write it down.
- Ponder why some of the teachers in our study lacked a purpose. Why should purpose be discussed in school and teacher education?
- Table 9 shows how many teachers associated their purpose in life with teaching. Think about this issue. Is teaching your purpose in life? Why?
- Become familiar with Figure 6, which presents teachers' evaluations of how they support their students' purpose in life. Ponder what factors could explain the differences between Finnish and Iranian teachers. How would you teach purpose to your students? Evaluate your approach with the items presented in Figure 6.
- Ponder the meaning of helping in the teaching profession. What does helping mean in a teaching context? Whom is the teacher helping?
- Study the didactical model presented in Figure 7. Try it in practice to support your own learning and advance your students' learning.
- Familiarize yourself with the pedagogical approaches presented by Malin (2018) in her book *Teaching for Purpose: Preparing Students for Lives of Meaning*. Choose one approach that you would like to try. Discuss the approaches in a group and develop new ones.
- Become familiar with the part of Table 10 (Moran) that presents the profiles in relation to the realization of purpose and the beyond-the-self dimension. In which profile would you locate yourself?
- Become familiar with the purpose profiles of Finnish students (Figure 8) and compare them with the American results. What could explain the similarities and differences between the profiles of Finnish and American youth?
- Become familiar with the types of purpose mentioned in Figure 9. Which are the most important for you? You can compare your answers with the results of students reported in this chapter. How do purposes differ among Finnish, US and Brazilian youth? What do young people in different cultures think about making the world a better place?

From Teachers' Implicit Beliefs to Ethical Actions

The previous chapter emphasized resilience through purposeful teaching in teachers' ethics. In this chapter, we argue that it is important to guide teachers to reflect on their implicit beliefs related to possible stereotypes in their thinking. In inclusive education, teachers' task is to provide equal learning opportunities to all students, including those with learning difficulties, immigrant backgrounds, specific talents, diverse gender identities, and various worldviews. We have developed a *growth mindset pedagogy* to help teachers actualize ethical teaching in inclusive classrooms by paying attention to implicit student beliefs that hinder their learning. We provide concrete examples of how teachers' have adopted a growth mindset pedagogy in their teaching and moral education. We also offer examples of teachers with entity beliefs (fixed mindset), i.e., teachers who believe that certain students are incapable of learning and who, thus, fail to invest time and effort in helping them. Such teachers might not understand the ethical nature of their profession and the implications of their implicit beliefs.

1   Teachers' Reflection on Their Beliefs and Actions

In Finnish teacher education, the goal is to educate teachers who can think ethically and pedagogically and reflect on their own work (Kansanen et al., 2000). Reflection is a necessary professional skill for educators to grow as teachers. The concept of reflection originates from John Dewey (1859–1952), who is also known for his philosophy of *learning by doing*. According to Dewey, reflection is 'active, persistent and careful consideration of any belief or supposed form of knowledge in the light of the grounds that support it, and further conclusions to which it leads' (Dewey, 1910, p. 6).

Teacher education includes both theoretical and practical studies. In teaching practice, the teacher learns by teaching, but this is insufficient; a teacher who thinks pedagogically also requires the skills to reflect on and justify the goals and acts of teaching. Donald Schön (1930–1997) transformed Dewey's definition of reflection into a schema for describing reflective practice. Schön identified *reflection-in-action* as a teacher's thinking during the teaching event, where decisions are quickly and often intuitively taken. By contrast, *reflection-on-action* refers, for example, to deeply pondering the goals achieved during class after the teaching event (Schön, 1983). In Finland, a teacher's professional skills also include guiding students toward reflection on obtaining new skills and knowledge (FNBE, 2016).

Teachers' professional ethics concern the commitment to support the development of every student. Teachers should believe that a student can learn even if the student lacks this belief or is not dedicated to studying. In an inclusive school, teachers encounter diverse students with different learning (dis)abilities, cultural backgrounds and socioemotional challenges. Teachers must continuously ponder how to distribute their time and resources between students. This decision requires teachers to understand the role and meaning of implicit beliefs for their ethical actions. Thus, it is useful for teachers to *know* the concepts of incremental beliefs (growth mindset) and entity beliefs (fixed mindset) presented in Carol Dweck's (2000, 2006) theory. Moreover, they could *reflect on* how these beliefs are manifested in their teaching and their students' learning.

As mentioned above, Dweck (2000, 2006) identifies two different implicit beliefs (mindsets) that guide our motivation, thinking and action. A teacher with a growth mindset believes that basic human qualities such as ability, intelligence and morality are malleable and can be developed, whereas a teacher with a fixed mindset believes that such qualities are stable and unalterable. According to growth mindset thinking, learning is a lifelong journey, and learning from mistakes is always possible. Fixed mindset thinking takes the opposite stand on these issues and advocates a belief that intelligence and giftedness are fixed at birth and cannot be developed. In this kind of thinking, a person's earlier accomplishments predict the possibilities for the future, and it is more difficult to learn from mistakes and change.

In her empirical research, Dweck (2000, pp. 119, 129) highlights the correlation between these mindsets and many areas of life. Mindsets can, for example, be connected to morality. Fixed mindset thinking leads easily to hiding mistakes, embellishment and lying. By contrast, growth mindset thinking encourages truthfulness, as only honest feedback helps the learner to advance. In Finnish studies, the majority of teachers possess a growth mindset related to the development of intelligence, giftedness and personality (Kuusisto & Tirri, 2013; Laine et al., 2016; Zhang et al., 2020a). However, in conceptions related to giftedness, we found a difference between teachers and parents (Kuusisto & Tirri, 2013). The teachers in our first study were more likely than the parents to consider giftedness a developmental attribute. Moreover, fixed mindset thinking was most prominent among parents from low socio-economic neighborhoods (Kuusisto & Tirri, 2013). However, when parents of the same low socio-economic school were studied five years later, most advocated a growth mindset (Tirri & Kuusisto, 2019), demonstrating a positive shift in parents' attitudes.

2   Implications of Teachers' Implicit Beliefs in Moral Education

In our empirical study on Finnish teachers' morality, we found qualitative differences among teachers related to their implicit beliefs on the possibilities of their students to develop as moral citizens and how they taught morality in their classrooms (Rissanen et al., 2018a). Moreover, in a previous study with four subject teachers in Finnish secondary schools (grades 7–9, I–III), we investigated the implications of teachers' mindsets for moral education, in particular the implications for *teaching morally* and *teaching morality* (Fenstermacher et al., 2009). The four teachers were chosen from a survey measuring Finnish teachers' (N = 463) mindsets using Carol Dweck's (2000) mindset inventory. The qualitative data included preliminary interviews with the four teachers, observations and videotaping of their classroom teaching (approximately 15 h per teacher), followed by stimulated recall interviews. Two of the teachers were identified as supporting a fixed mindset (Jack, Patsy) and two a growth mindset (Kate, Sally).

Jack, mathematics teacher, displayed a tendency towards a fixed mindset when teaching morally. In the interview, he described his idea of the teaching profession in the following way:

> I do not think about my work from an ethical point of view. I think that teaching does not need any ethics. It can only be teaching of the subject. The teacher is not necessarily an ethical exemplar, they can be only teachers. (Jack, preliminary interview)

Jack ignored the ethical aspects of teaching, instead concentrating on his duties to teach mathematics as a subject and helping students learn the content. He separated moral roles from teachers' roles, seeing teaching as only transforming knowledge and skills.

Jack's tendency towards a fix mindset was also reflected in his views on teaching morality. In his opinion it was no longer possible to foster students' moral growth in secondary school. According to Jack, it was too late to teach moral behavior. Thus, he demonstrated helplessness responses to students' moral growth.

> Let's say … it is very difficult to aim at the personal development of the students. Mostly, we try to keep them under some kind of control. At this phase, in upper comprehensive school, it is not possible to teach manners that much anymore; I cannot regard that as my responsibility anymore, whether they wear hats in the classroom, spit on the streets, wait at traffic lights, stay quiet in the classroom … even though in my lessons, of

course, I take care of that. But it's like ... their behavior, they have already learned it, and you cannot change it anymore. (Jack, preliminary interview, Rissanen et al., 2018b, p. 72)

Our previous empirical research also identified deficits among preservice teachers and practicing mathematics teachers in understanding the holistic nature of the teaching profession, including ethical sensitivity (Kuusisto et al., 2012). Nevertheless, in Finland both the national curriculum and teachers' professional ethics emphasize the holistic nature of teaching, including students' moral development. All teachers, regardless of their subjects, thus require education in how to include an ethical dimension in their teaching.

Kate, a language teacher, tended towards a growth mindset. Her ethical conduct and ethos indicated a humanistic worldview that was in line with that of the Finnish teachers' ethical code, which is based on humanistic psychology and human rights. In the next interview extract, she emphasizes the individual needs and rights of students with the goal of making the world a better place through her teaching.

I think what actually motivates me the most in teaching languages is that, in the end, the aim of learning languages is that there would be no wars, no hatred, because language helps you to come closer to other human beings who do not share your culture. (Kate, preliminary interview, Rissanen et al., 2018b, p. 69)

Kate was also motivated to teach ethics to her students. For example, during one of the lessons we observed, a student arrived late for the second consecutive time. This is how Kate responded:

So is there a problem with your alarm clock? This is the second time you've shown up late. If the reason is; I'm sorry, but I assume the reason is that you're on the computer too late in the evening, so cut it out. I mean come on; it is the middle of the day already. I woke up at six today and so have many others here; so I will send a message to your parents about this; they have to know about this. (Kate, critical incident 41, Rissanen et al., 2018b, p. 70)

In the stimulated recall interview, Kate justified her actions in the following way:

Well, that was a bit mean of me, but I don't think it's that bad that I say these things, because it's not the result of your appearance, but what

you do or don't do. That's what I criticize. I don't even know the families of these students, like, 'your brother was terrible, and I've taught
your mother and she was terrible too, always late' .... I know people have
heard these things, that you will never achieve anything because your
dad didn't either .... I would never fall for that kind of thinking. (Kate,
stimulated recall interview, Rissanen et al., 2018b, p. 70)

Thus, Kate focused on the student's ethical actions with emphasis on situational attributions, rather than family background, in facing ethical conflicts
and challenges. She was motivated to enhance students' ethical growth. The
implications of teachers' mindsets for teaching ethics and teaching ethically
are compiled in Table 11.

In a study among American and Finnish upper secondary students, we were
able to use a short intervention to change the mindsets of students related to

TABLE 11   Implications of teachers' mindsets for teaching morally and teaching morality
            (from Rissanen et al., 2018b, p. 66)

	Tendencies related to teachers' fixed mindset	Tendencies related to teachers' growth mindset
Professional moral ethos of teachers ('Teaching morally')	– Fulfilling professional responsibilities and norms – Striving for justice – Duty-based morality	– Taking responsibility for students' personal development – Meeting individual needs and preserving individual rights – Rights-based morality
Educating students' ethical capabilities ('Teaching morality')	Fostering students' – Fixed mindset about morality – Dispositional attribu-tions of moral offenses – Maladaptive and ego-defensive courses of action when facing moral offenses and challenges – Helplessness responses to moral growth	Fostering students' – Growth mindset about morality – Situational attributions of moral offenses – Adaptive courses of action when facing moral conflicts and challenges – Motivation for moral growth

revenge in conflict situations. By studying growth-mindset thinking, students who desired revenge changed their mindsets and became ready to negotiate and search for more constructive solutions to conflicts with their peers (Yeager et al., 2011). Moreover, in Chile, the research findings of a national study demonstrated that growth-mindset thinking decreased the effects of poverty on secondary-school students' academic achievements (Claro et al., 2016). The presence of a growth mindset in a teacher's ethical thinking implies that all members of the school community can learn and develop new knowledge, skills and attitudes.

Dweck's theory is based on neurological studies demonstrating the potential of the brain to develop throughout a person's life. This quality is called neuroplasticity (Kujala & Näätänen, 2010). The brain can be viewed as a muscle that requires practice, repetition and challenges in order to develop and learn. With practice, new cells are created in the brain with new connections, synapses. This means that learning has a strong biological foundation. Moreover, it indicates that intelligence, giftedness, and morality can be developed. All this implies that implicit beliefs important part of teachers' reflection in both pre- and in-service education.

3   Manifestations of Teacher's Implicit Beliefs in Teaching – The Case of Anne

Anne is an elementary school teacher specialized in teaching first and second grades. She is highly experienced also in supervising preservice teachers in their teaching practicum. At the time of the study, Anne taught a first-grade class with seven-year-old students.

For the research, Anne first completed Dweck's inventory (Table 12). This was followed by observation and videotaping of her teaching for one week (19 hours). The purpose of the observation was to explore how implicit beliefs are manifested in teaching (See Rissanen et al., 2019). According to the results from Dweck's inventory, Anne displayed both growth-mindset and fixed-mindset tendences in her thinking, indicating a mixed mindset (Rissanen et al., 2019).

The video recordings of Anne's teaching demonstrated that she strongly emphasized learning processes, which is a central feature of a growth mindset pedagogy (Rissanen et al., 2019). Anne typically provided positive feedback praising her students. Her feedback systematically focused on effort, completing tasks, and choosing strategies. For example, when a student had finished a task quickly, Anne asked the student to describe how they had found the solution: 'How did you came up with this result? How did you reason it?'

TABLE 12   Mindsets manifested in Anne's teaching

Teacher Anne	Fixed mindset	Growth mindset
Mindsets about learning		
Dweck's inventory	Intelligence ($M = 3.0$)	Giftedness ($M = 3.75$)
Definition in own words	Giftedness is an inherent ability to master certain areas of life	Without work and effort, giftedness will narrow
Mindsets actualizing in teaching		
Noticing individual needs of the students	– Emphasis on successes – Traits and gifts of talented students are stable – Persistence and learning-to-learn skills taught to students with learning difficulties	– Focus on learning and process – Knowing one's students and noticing their individual – No tests or exams, in order to keep the focus on learning and to avoid students defining themselves or their learning with test results.
Feedback	Anne wanted to encourage gifted and talented students to trust themselves more, but she did not identify these students' need for special support to encounter their challenges	– Praising effort and strategies – Anne did not praise students for completing tasks quickly. Instead, she asked them to describe how they found the solution
Attitude towards mistakes	– Avoiding random mistakes – Anne aimed to anticipate and prevent students' mistakes if she thought they would cause emotional distress – Learning by mistakes was only allowed for students who could cope with failure	– Mistakes are part of the learning process – It is important for students to see that the teacher also fails

Anne's questions helped students verbalize their thinking process. This kind of process feedback has been found to be the best way to support learning motivation and students' positive inner talk. It also helps students cope better and avoid self-criticism if and when they subsequently make mistakes (Kamins & Dweck, 1999).

Furthermore, Anne's focus on learning and mastery was evident in her decision not to use exams or tests to evaluate her students' learning. In her experience, test results easily caused students to define themselves both as students and human beings. Anne wanted her students to concentrate on developing and learning rather than performing or comparing themselves to others. Anne's pedagogical strategies embodied the principles of the Finnish National Core Curriculum (FNBE, 2016), which highlight learning processes and evaluation based on students' own previous work rather than comparison with students.

Anne emphasized the importance of teachers knowing their students well in order to meet their diverse needs and guide their individual learning processes. Anne's goal was to tailor teaching and tasks to match the developmental level of each student. Moreover, she strove to choose tasks that enabled her to encounter and support each student at an individual level. Thus, Anne's pedagogical thinking and actions were mostly in line with a growth mindset pedagogy, and educational policy in Finland.

Anne seemed to acknowledge the importance of making mistakes in learning. Indeed, she wanted her students to see that even teachers could make mistakes:

> Often, I make mistakes by accident, but sometimes I make them on purpose, so that the children can see their teacher perhaps does not always know things …. I try to communicate that mistakes are ok and it's not so serious if you make them and somehow through that encourage them, like, let's just do this again and let's give it another try. (Anne, preliminary interview, Rissanen et al., 2019, p. 209)

Anne hoped for and anticipated mistakes beforehand in order to challenge her students' thinking. Thus, she used failures and conflicts as pedagogical tools.

> I tried to create an intellectual conflict – this was a very fruitful situation and I was really happy when I noticed that they put them in pairs [differently shaped pieces of paper], but all the pieces did not have a pair – of course I could not have arranged this beforehand, but I was hoping this would happen. (Anne, critical incident 1, stimulated recall interview)

By contrast, Anne did not seem to permit random failures. On the contrary, she aimed to prevent mistakes, especially when she thought students would be unable to cope or when they might cause students stress and anxiety. For example, during one Finnish language lesson, students were working in small groups, with group members placed in alphabetical order according to various criteria. This time, students were asked to arrange themselves in alphabetical order based on the first letter of their last names. When the group was ready, they raised their hands to ask Anne to check their order. When she asked what letters their lasts names began with, one student failed to reply. Eventually, the other students helped find the answer, and Anne ignored the problem by assigning the group a new principle with which to organize themselves in alphabetical order. Anne commented on this situation as follows:

> Since it was January [indicating almost six months of schooling], I was hoping that the student would have said something or at least looked at me. Eventually. [This student is] incredibly talented, but I do not usually ask her anything if I kind of sense that she does not want to answer. She wants to feel somehow very sure [before she is willing to answer]. (Anne, critical incident 15, stimulated recall interview)

Anne was very sensitive towards her students' emotional states, and, when she noticed uncertainty, she wished to avoid exposing her student to possible failures. In the preliminary interview, Anne had described the same student in the following way:

> For example, I have one student who is ridiculously talented; she can do absolutely everything, and I do not even know how much she can, since she is so shy and cautious. For her, encouragement like 'just say now' or something like that does not work. So, I have been thinking that she kind of gathers courage and then at some point, since she is so smart, then at some point she will dare to show it a little bit. (Anne, preliminary interview)

Anne wished to encourage talented students to trust themselves, and she provided them space to gather their courage. At the same time, however, she decided not to attempt to help these students practice failing and coping with failure in a safe environment.

Anne's class also contained another academically talented student who could not tolerate mistakes. Moreover, he seemed to lack persistence. In addition, Anne had noticed that this student was overly self-confident, which was evident when he refused all help from the teacher. Anne wished to be extremely sensitive with this student too and was reluctant to challenge him or attempt to change his unhelpful belief systems. Instead, Anne seemed to trust in the stability of the traits, such as intelligence and giftedness, in talented students (see also Kärkkäinen & Räty, 2010). She did not consider that these students might need the teacher's guidance in the emotional domain. Anne's choice is understandable, since in Finnish schools academically talented students often lacking guidance and help. They are not offered challenges in which they can take risks, process their fear of failure, learn to cope with unpleasant emotions and turn difficulties into learning opportunities (Laine & Tirri, 2016; Rissanen et al., 2018a, 2019; Tirri & Kuusisto, 2013).

4 Promoting Equal Opportunities with a Growth Mindset Pedagogy

A growth mindset pedagogy promotes equal opportunities for all students to learn in inclusive schools. Table 13 presents the cornerstones of a growth mindset pedagogy, which are supporting individual learning processes, mastery

TABLE 13 Growth mindset pedagogy (from Rissanen et al., 2019, p. 206)

Supporting individual learning processes	Supporting mastery orientation
– Avoiding quick, stereotypical judgements of students	– Fostering learning goals
– Frequent one-on-one interactions with students	– Emphasis on formative assessment
– Learning about individual students' barriers to learning and helping students overcome them	– Avoiding comparisons with other students
– Differentiation as the basis of pedagogical practice	
Fostering students' process-focused thinking	**Persistence**
– Praising courage, strategies, effort	– Not giving up on students and leaving no room for helpless behavior patterns
– Teaching the positive role of failures, mistakes, and challenges in learning	– Not protecting students from challenges
– Fostering students' incremental beliefs and situational attributions	– Honest critical feedback in the form of 'not yet'
– Teaching learning strategies and emphasizing learning-to-learn goals	

orientation in learning, enhancement of process-oriented thinking and teachers' persistence.

Supporting individual learning processes means that teachers avoid deliberately labelling their students and their learning, skills or character. Even though teachers need to make diagnostic observations, the starting point does not reveal what the student could learn or define the learning process and its aims. In order to support students' growth in the best possible way, teachers with growth mindsets highlight knowing and individually interacting with their students. In this way, teachers can learn to identify individual barriers and learning pits and help students overcome them. Differentiated teaching is one of the main tools for supporting individual learning processes (Laine & Tirri, 2016).

A growth mindset pedagogy emphasizes *mastery orientation in learning.* This means that the teacher underlines *learning goals* rather than *performance goals.* The aim is to learn, understand, and master in line with Bloom's taxonomy. In addition, the teacher makes the subject personally meaningful, indicating that studying is not merely superficial and repetitive. In this kind of process, formative assessment that supports learning and avoids comparisons with peers during the whole process is important.

Benjamin Bloom's (1913–1999) famous taxonomy of educational goals helps plan, evaluate and reflect on teaching and learning. Bloom developed the taxonomy to describe the six stages in cognitive development (see Figure 11).

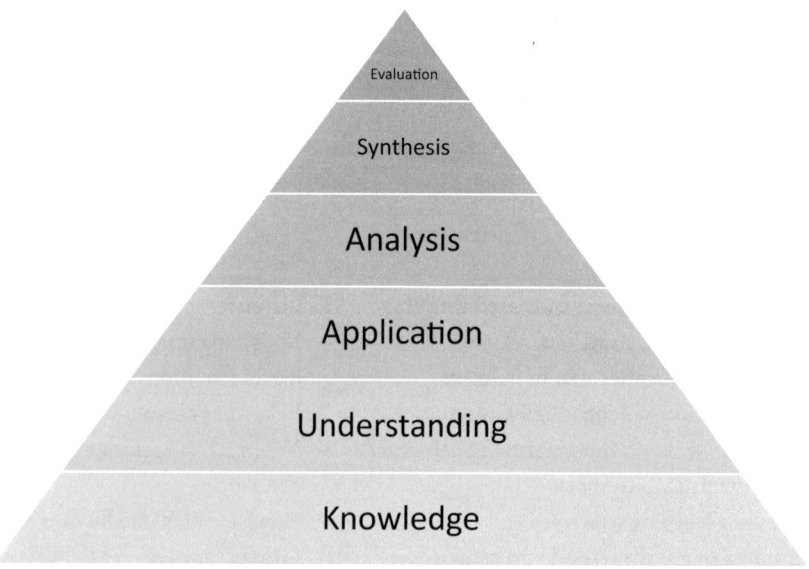

FIGURE 11   The stages in Bloom's taxonomy (from Bloom et al., 1956)

1. At the lowest stage of the taxonomy, *knowing*, the goal of learning is to identify and repeat, to show knowledge of the task in learning. A student can list, repeat, describe, define, identify and label.
2. At the stage of *understanding*, the goal of education is to understand the meaning and purpose of the knowledge and demonstrate this understanding. A student can explain, summarize, interpret, estimate, annotate and categorize.
3. At the stage of *applying*, the goal of learning is to use the knowledge in new situations and demonstrate the practical application of this skill. A student can choose, integrate, judge, execute and present.
4. At the stage of *analyzing*, the goal of learning is to dissect knowledge and categorize it according to its most essential characteristics. A student can analyze, debate, divide and generalize.
5. At the stage of *synthesizing*, the goal of learning is to present creative and unique solutions and create holistic frameworks. A student can create, plan, produce and synthesize.
6. At the stage of *evaluating*, the goal of learning is to create and develop criteria for assessing knowledge and developing critical thinking. A student can compare, reason, contrast, create criteria and evaluate.

Bloom's taxonomy can be used in the evaluation of the teaching-studying-learning process. In *summative evaluations*, the taxonomy is used to support the final and numerical evaluation. In *formative evaluations*, continuous qualitative feedback is provided for the advancement of the student. In *diagnostic evaluations*, the stage of a student's learning is identified at the beginning of a course or studies. The Finnish National Core Curriculum for Basic Education (FNBE, 2016) encourages the teacher to evaluate and give feedback in multiple ways and support students' self-reflection.

The stages of Bloom's taxonomy guide teachers and students to reflect on how well students master the learning content. In this way, teaching provides the best possibilities for a student to create different meanings from the content taught. For example, in religious education, studying only at the stage of knowledge leads a student to memorize facts about different religions (for example, 'the Pope is the leader of the Catholic church'). The meaning of religion, however, is not elucidated only at the stage of knowledge, as this stage does not include the significance of the Pope for those committed to the Catholic church. At the stage of evaluation, instead, students can reflect on the meaning of religious leadership for different churches and religions, evaluate the role of religion in society and form their own opinion on religious leadership. Understanding and evaluating these meanings does not require a person to belong to the Catholic church or to be a believer or religious. However, critical reflection and choosing a stand are crucial in all school subjects and in supporting the holistic development of the student (FNBE, 2016).

Supporting students' process-centered thinking refers mainly to the teacher's feedback style. Positive comments should be provided on courage, choosing strategies and effort. Students should be taught the importance to learning of challenges and mistakes. Failures are not disasters but opportunities to learn. For example, in a mathematics class, the teacher should compliment students for making mistakes: 'how many mistakes did you make and what did you learn from them?' (Boaler, 2019). This creates a more open approach to learning where challenges are seen as positive, even crucial, aspects of the process. Students can be taught the meaning of growth and fixed mindsets in an age-appropriate way. Consequently, students learn concepts that help them understand and self-regulate their own learning process. For instance, students can be taught to ponder whether they explain and attribute their learning and challenges to a growth mindset approach, in other words, to factors they can influence, such as choosing strategies and making an effort, or to a fixed mindset approach, in other words to factors they cannot impact.

A growth mindset pedagogy highlights a teacher's *persistence*, which means that the teacher is committed to supporting students' learning processes and perseveres irrespective of success or failure. Here, teachers can be demanding, expect good behavior and request that students also invest in studying. Teachers with a growth mindset tendences provide honest feedback and use the expression 'not yet.' The following example shows how a teacher's persistent use of 'not yet' changes a student's own inner talk and helps him self-regulate his actions (Ronkainen et al., 2019, pp. 147–148):

> Many of the first graders become impatient at the beginning of the autumn when they are not able to do things. For example, Henri was not able to read or write at all [when he started first grade], so he used to say very often 'I cannot do this.' And what the child means by that is that 'I am not going to do this because I cannot because it is very hard and challenging.' So, I have started or I willingly hasten to add: 'You cannot do it yet.' I always like to add the word 'yet' to students' sentences. And then sometimes I will continue by saying 'the reason why we practice is so you will learn this.' And guess what? Once I almost started crying when Henri was doing some exercise, and he was murmuring to himself: 'This is the dumbest exercise because I cannot do it yet,' and he didn't realize that he was saying that, but he just kept on working. (Mari, critical incident 6, stimulated recall interview)

Teachers require education in the implementation of a growth mindset pedagogy. In our recent study, five elementary school teachers participated in design-based research to learn the principles of a growth mindset pedagogy and co-create an educational program based on these principles. Those teachers with a growth mindset seemed to internalize the principles of a growth mindset pedagogy more deeply than did teachers with fixed-mindset tendencies (Rissanen et al., 2021). Thus, it is important to pay attention to teachers own mindset tendencies and the dangers of superficial understandings of a growth mindset during teacher education.

Certain limitations exist to the implementation of a growth mindset pedagogy that stem from the national curriculum and school environment. For example, in our study involving principals in Finland and Estonia, a Finnish principal identified evaluation as a difficult area in which to manifest such a pedagogy. In lower secondary education, teachers are required to assign grades to students that enable them to proceed to future studies. This practice forces students to focus more on their grades than on their own learning goals (Tirri et al., 2021).

Teachers and schools require support from homes and parents to implement a growth mindset pedagogy. Parents are important partners in creating a school community with shared values and strategies. Students' peers also play crucial role in creating growth-mindset learning communities in schools (Zhang et al., 2020b). In a study involving Finnish (n = 870) and Chinese (n = 992) secondary school students, we found that the way students praise their peers in their feedback primes and modifies their mindsets and academic motivation (Zhang et al., 2020b). The opportunity for students to provide feedback should thus be included in courses at all grade levels. Teacher education should also include education on how to guide students to give process-oriented feedback to their peers. The implication is that it is insufficient merely to teach mindset theory in schools or teacher education; instead, practical applications are required (Zhang et al., 2020b).

5   Questions to Reflect on by Yourself or with Your Peers

- Where does the concept of reflection come from? What experiences do you have of reflection? Discuss those experiences.
- How is a growth mindset related to morality? How can a teacher use a growth mindset pedagogy in moral education?
- How do you see the learning potential of diverse students? Can every student learn everything?

– Study the stages of Bloom's taxonomy. Which have you utilized most in your own studying and teaching?
– Reflect on the areas in life where you believe in growth mindset thinking, i.e., the idea of being able to grow and develop.
– Reflect on the areas in life where fixed mindset-thinking prevents you from growing and learning new things.
– How can you adopt a growth mindset to facilitate your own growth and the education of your students?
– Become familiar with Anne's thinking and ponder how you could strengthen a growth mindset pedagogy in her teaching.
– Table 13 shows the main points of a growth mindset pedagogy. Which of these factors are the most challenging for you in teaching and why? Which of the factors do you think you master already, and which factors should you practice more?
– The example in this section involves a first-grade student, Henri, who experienced learning and concentration difficulties. What kind of pedagogy and pedagogical strategies would you use to help Henri?
– How can principals support a growth mindset pedagogy in schools? What kind of opportunities and challenges do principals face in implementing a growth mindset pedagogy?
– What is parents' role in supporting a growth mindset in their children?
– What can peers do to support each other's learning?

Building Moral Communities in Schools

This book has explored the teaching profession from an ethical standpoint by discussing multiple ethical frameworks and concrete challenges. In Finland, teaching is seen as an ethical profession with high quality academic education and ethical code. The ethical code and national curriculum provide a value base and common goals for teaching and learning. Finnish teachers enjoy the freedom and responsibility to plan, realize and evaluate their own teaching in an appropriate manner for diverse students. In this book, we have argued that no single ethical framework provides concrete answers to the ethical challenges teachers encounter in their work. Instead, teachers should reflect on multiple ethical frameworks to learn their professional ethics. The previous chapters have described the skills a teacher requires to become an ethical professional. We have explored models and pedagogical ideas to support ethical teaching. In addition, we have argued that ethical sensitivity, purposeful teaching, and a growth mindset in learning are prerequisites for ethical teaching.

Finnish teachers are ethical professionals who are committed to the ethical principles of their profession and the values underlying them. Ethical teaching is based on teachers' professional identity, including the goal to facilitate the personal development of students. In order to support students' holistic development, educators must share a common value base and be committed to mutual goals in their school communities. One concrete way for teachers to show commitment to their profession is to take Comenius' Oath in the same way that students graduating as medical doctors take the Hippocratic Oath at their graduation ceremony. Taking the oath emphasizes professional ethics as part of a teacher's professional identity.

Teachers require both pedagogical and ethical skills in their work. We have emphasized ethical sensitivity as an important skill that helps teachers identify ethical issues in their own work and school community. Ethical sensitivity is also necessary in interaction between the different partners with whom a teacher cooperates. Ethical sensitivity helps a teacher read and express different emotions, care by connecting to others, work with interpersonal and group differences, adopt the perspective of others, prevent social bias and identify the consequences of actions and options. With the different cases and perspectives presented in this book, teachers can evaluate their own ethical sensitivity related to their current challenges (see Chapter 4).

© KONINKLIJKE BRILL NV, LEIDEN, 2022 | DOI:10.1163/9789004532649_007

Ethical sensitivity is a skill that can be learned and developed. We found caring by connecting to others to be the most central dimension in teachers' ethical sensitivity in all the countries we investigated (Finland, Estonia, and Iran). This aspect of ethical sensitivity can be seen as culturally invariant. On the other hand, adopting the perspective of others was found to be a culturally dependent skill. Teachers should possess knowledge of cultural differences to help them understand families from different backgrounds. Understanding increases ethical sensitivity in teachers' work.

The goal of the teaching profession is to help students grow and develop as whole individuals. In this holistic task, teachers are required to reflect on a purpose in life together with their students. This book has defined a purpose in life as a long-term goal that is meaningful to individuals themselves and directed also beyond the self. Teaching can represent such a purpose for many teachers. Educators who have found a long-term goal in teaching and have made a longstanding commitment to support their students can be termed purposeful teachers. Purposeful teachers possess a clear understanding what they wish to achieve in teaching and the justifications for these goals. The goal of a purposeful teacher is well aligned with the ideal of a teacher who thinks pedagogically. Such teachers are aware of the values and goals of the curriculum and realize them in their teaching.

The current national curriculum in Finland encourages students to reflect on their purposes and the consequences of their choices and lifestyles. Education is focused on the future by nurturing the persistence of students. For instance, the choices taken today should be investigated from the perspective of sustainable development. Teachers play an important role in helping their students find a long-term and stable purpose for their lives. Teaching goals include reflection on the meaning and significance of different subjects with students. The didactic skills of a teacher include the ability to help students find the personal relevance of the subject studied. Chapter 5 presented a didactical model that teachers can use in guiding their students to reflect on and analyze their own purposeful teaching or learning experiences.

Many previous studies have profiled Finland as a country where individuality is emphasized more than communality. Our findings reported in Chapter 5 confirm this notion. Both Finnish students' and teachers' purposes in life were mainly self-oriented. For the majority of teachers, teaching was not a component of their purpose in life. Nevertheless, teaching provided teachers with happiness and the opportunity for development and self-actualization. Moreover, some teachers regarded helping children and young people as a highly important goal that matched their personal aims in life. Finnish ethical guidelines for teachers emphasize teamwork and the communality of the teaching profession. In the same way, the national curriculum presents the goal of creating learning communities in which members study and learn together.

In order to support the holistic development of students, a teacher must believe in their potential to grow and develop. A growth mindset in teaching emphasizes the developmental potential of each student. The teacher's task is to diagnose the current developmental phase of the student and provide appropriate challenges and help. By tailoring their teaching, educators can support diverse students. Remedial teaching is required, for example, with low-achieving students, while high-achieving students can be taught with more challenging tasks and various teaching methods.

Morality is present in the teaching of all subjects and grade levels. Teachers are always role models for their students. Teaching morally refers to a teacher's moral ethos in teaching. It includes both the entire morality of a teacher's conduct and modelling morally valuable behavior to the students. In Chapter 6, teaching morally was demonstrated with the help of case studies. Here, a teacher with growth mindset tendencies demonstrated how she took responsibility for students' moral development and their individual needs.

We have developed a growth mindset pedagogy that emphasizes teachers' persistence in supporting individual learning processes, process-focused thinking, and mastery orientation in students. A growth mindset pedagogy provides the ethical foundation for teachers' work to meet the individual needs of all their students. However, it is insufficient that teachers alone practice a growth mindset pedagogy; rather, it is important that the whole school community, principals, parents and students, is committed to the principles of this pedagogy. In building moral communities, we need a shared pedagogical vision with a strong ethical basis.

Building moral communities in schools requires commitment from all members of the community, including students, parents, other staff members and various partners. For teachers, this is supported by ethical codes that emphasizes communality and collegiality. The school also requires critical friends to provide new perspectives on its moral discourse. These relationships epitomize the African saying 'it takes the whole village to educate a child.' The school is a moral community where the ethics of both the teacher and the whole community are important. Thus, the ethical thinking of the entire learning community should be promoted.

This book has presented concrete ways to deal with moral conflicts in schools. For instance, in roundtable discussions (Chapter 3), teachers are responsible for creating a situation where all members of the learning community are able to communicate, listen to each other and jointly search for the best solutions. Teachers operate as engaged participants and demonstrate through their actions that they expect everybody involved to take responsibility, search for truth, decide freely and integrate aspects of truthfulness, caring and justice into their choices. Moreover, the teacher should trust in advance that the members will find a solution that is in the best interest of school community.

This book has presented the current challenges related to teachers' professional ethics with empirical data gathered from Finland and abroad. Teachers are always educators for the future. This perspective should be present in teacher education from first-year studies to in-service education. Teachers are committed to life-long learning and professional development. Changes in society always raise new challenges that the teacher must meet. Different kinds of families challenge teachers to reflect on how they can meet the needs of diverse students through integration and differentiated teaching. In all these professional solutions, teachers can lean on strong professional ethics, which also provide a purpose for teaching.

Ethical Code of Finnish Teachers

Teachers' Values and Ethical Principles (Trade Union of Education in Finland, 2010)

Ethical principles of teaching

Teaching is an independent profession and a demanding expert task that inherently involves professional ethics. The key aspects of teachers' ethical principles are presented in the ethical principles for the teaching profession.

The teaching profession requires that those working as a teacher comply with a high standard of professional ethics and that society can trust that teachers act ethically in all situations.

Teacher's expertise and values

Responsibility related to a teacher's work is based on know-how and the work's values and norms. Neither of these can replace the other: poor expertise does not compensate for good ethical principles and vice versa.

Teachers must continuously maintain their expertise, have special sensitivity to recognise the ethical dilemmas involved in teaching work and the readiness to act ethically in these situations.

Separating legal and ethical issues

Legal and ethical issues must be treated separately in teachers' ethics. Although a teacher's basic task and responsibilities are defined in legislation and standards, professional ethics cannot be based on compulsion or external control. Instead, professional ethics are based on a teacher's internalised understanding of the profession's moral demands.

Societal expectations

The results of a teacher's work are often not seen until much later. Good learning experiences support life-long learning, and teachers play a significant role in creating a positive learning experience and in strengthening the learner's confidence and sense of social responsibility. A teacher's job is to improve the opportunities for education, teaching and learning for the benefit of the individual. Teachers are expected to meet society's expectations, which concern the actualization of the teaching goals. Due to societal changes, many teachers are forced to deal many matters in their work for which they cannot hold sole responsibility.

© KONINKLIJKE BRILL NV, LEIDEN, 2022 | DOI:10.1163/9789004532649_008

The power and responsibility of a teacher

The shift in the role of teachers has brought the teacher closer to the learner. It adds to the teacher's responsibility for the learner's development and often also requires co-operation with other parties responsible for the learner's development. Assessment of the learner is closely linked to the teacher's power and responsibility. Internalised ethics prevent teachers from misusing their position.

Teacher's values and ethical principles

The core of teaching consists of four basic values: dignity, truthfulness, fairness and responsibility & freedom. All teaching is founded on ethics – whether it be the teacher-student relationship, pluralism or a teacher's relationship with their work.
Dignity means respect for humanity. Teachers must respect every person, regardless of gender, sexual orientation, gender diversity, appearance, age, religion, social standing, origin, opinions, abilities and achievements.
Truthfulness is one of the core values in teachers' basic task, which involves steering learners in navigating life and their environment. Honesty with oneself and others and mutual respect in all communication is a basic aspect of teachers' work.
Fairness is important both when encountering individual learners and groups but also in the work community. Fairness involves in particular promoting equality and non-discrimination and avoiding favouritism.
Teachers are entitled to their own values, but in their work, teachers' responsibility is tied to their basic task and its standards such as legislation and the curriculum.

Teacher's ethical principles

The aim of teachers' ethical principles is to draw attention to the ethics involved in teaching.
Good professional ethics are among a teacher's most important resources.
Teachers and relationship with work
Teachers commit to the standards and ethics of their work. Teachers manage their duties responsibly. Teachers develop their work and expertise and assess their own actions. Teachers teach in a manner that reflects their personality, so developing and caring for their individuality is their right and obligation. Teachers are entitled to be treated fairly in their work.

Teachers and learners

Teachers accept and treat learners as unique human beings. Teachers respect the rights of learners and react to them humanely and fairly. Teachers try to understand the learners' starting point, thoughts and opinions. Teachers considerately handle matters linked to the learner's personality and privacy. Teachers pay special attention to learners who require care and protection and do not, under any circumstances, tolerate bullying or the abuse of other people. Teachers' work also includes teaching learners to co-operate and to become good members of society. Building up confidence and good relationships is part of teachers' work.

Teachers and the work community

Teachers value their work and respect their colleagues. Teachers try to pool their resources and find a balance between their autonomy and the work community. Accepting the individuality of colleagues, understanding them and helping and supporting each other are key principles of the work community.

Teachers and society

Teaching is one of the most important jobs in society. Teachers' ability to be effective in their work and take care of their professional development are dependent not only on their commitment, but also on the resources allocated to teaching and education. Teachers promote the opportunities offered by education and growth. Teachers represent, above all, learners' rights and interests – even critically, if necessary. In their work, they also teach learners to become responsible members of a democratic society.

Teachers and stakeholders

Teachers work together with learners' parents, guardians and other parties responsible for education, training and well-being. These include social and health care expert groups, authorities and numerous other collaborating parties. The co-operation supports learners' learning and development.

Teachers and plurality

Teachers need to ensure that all learners have the same rights and obligations as members of society. They make sure that learners and their parents' cultures and world views are respected equally and that no one is discriminated against based on them.

References

Airaksinen, T. (1998). Opettaja, arvot ja muuttuva ammatti [Teacher, values and changing profession]. In R. Sarras (Ed.), *Puheenvuoroja opettajan etiikasta* [*Statements about teacher ethics*] (pp. 5–13). Trade Union of Education in Finland.

Alexander, L., & Moore, M. (2020). Deontological ethics. In E. N. Zalta (Ed.), *The Stanford encyclopedia of philosophy* (Winter 2020 ed.). Retrieved May 4, 2021, from https://plato.stanford.edu/archives/win2020/entries/ethics-deontological/

Aristotle. (1975). *The Nicomachean ethics. Books I–X* (D. Ross, Trans.). Oxford University Press.

Bandura, A. (1991). Social cognitive theory of moral thought and action. In W. Kurtines & J. Gewirtz (Eds.), *Handbook of moral Behavior and development 1* (pp. 45–103). Lawrence Erlbaum Associates.

Bebeau, M., Rest, J., & Narvaez, D. (1999). Beyond the promise: A perspective on research in moral education. *Educational Researcher, 28*(4), 18–26.

Berliner, D. (1991). Educational psychology and pedagogical expertise: New findings and new opportunities for thinking about training. *Educational Psychologist, 26*(2), 145–55.

Bloom, B. S., Engelhart, M. D., Furst, E. J., Hill, W. H., & Krathwohl, D. R. (1956). *Taxonomy of educational objectives. The classification of educational goals. Handbook I: Cognitive domain.* David McKay Co.

Boaler, J. (2019). *Limitless mind.* Harper Collins.

Brabeck, M. M., Rogers, L. A., Sirin, S., Henderson, J., Benvenuto, M., & Weaver, M. (2000). Increasing ethical sensitivity to racial and gender intolerance in schools: Development of the racial ethical sensitivity test. *Ethics & Behavior, 10*(2), 119–137.

Bricker, D. (1993). Character and moral reasoning: An Aristotelian perspective. In K. Strike & P. L. Ternasky (Eds.), *Ethics for professionals in education. Perspectives for preparation and practice* (pp. 13–26). Teachers College Press.

Bronk, K. C. (2014). *Purpose in life. A critical component of optimal youth development.* Springer.

Bundick, M. J. (2011). The benefits of reflecting on and discussing purpose in life in emerging adulthood. *New Directions for Youth Development, 132*, 89–104.

Bundick, M. J., Andrews, M., Jones, A., Mariano, J. M., Bronk, K. C., & Damon, W. (2006). *Revised youth purpose survey.* Stanford Center on Adolescence.

Bundick, M. J., & Tirri, K. (2014). Student perceptions of teacher support and competencies for fostering youth purpose and positive youth development: Perspectives from two countries. *Applied Developmental Science, 18*(3), 148–162.

Campbell, E. (2003). *The ethical teacher.* Open University Press.

Clark, C. (1990). The teacher and the taught: Moral transactions in the classroom. In J. Goodlad, R. Soder, & K. Sirotnik (Eds.), *The moral dimensions of teaching* (pp. 251–265). Jossey-Bass.

Claro, S., Paunesku, D., & Dweck, C. S. (2016). Growth mindset tempers effects of poverty on academic achievement. *Psychological and Cognitive Sciences, 113*, 8664–8668.

Colby, A., & Kohlberg, L. (1987). *The measurement of moral judgement 1–2*. Cambridge University Press.

Comenius, J. A. (1896). *The great didactic of John Amos Comenius* (Didacta Magna) (M. W. Keatinge, Ed., Trans.). A. & C. Black (Original work published 1657). Retrieved May 4, 2021, from https://books.google.com/books/about/The_Great_Didactic_of_John_Amos_Comenius.html?id=sE9MAAAAIAAJ&printsec=frontcover&source=kp_read_button#v=onepage&q&f=false

Cvencek, D., Meltzoff, A. N., & Greenwald, A. (2011). Math–gender stereotypes in elementary school children. *Child Development, 82*(3), 766–779.

Damon, W. (1995). *Greater expectations. Overcoming the culture of indulgence in America's homes and schools*. Free Press.

Damon, W. (2008). *The path to purpose. Helping our children find their calling in life*. Simon & Schuster.

Damon, W., & Colby, A. (2015). *The power of ideals. The real story of moral choice*. Oxford University Press.

Damon, W., Moran, S., Tirri, K., Araujo, U., & Bundick, B. (2009, July 18–27). *Finding purpose in three societies. Cultural analysis in the United States, Finland, and Brazil* [Paper]. Conference of the International Positive Psychology Association, Philadelphia.

Darling-Hammond, L. (1990). Teacher professionalism: Why and how? In A. Lieberman (Ed.), *Schools as collaborative cultures. Creating the future now* (pp. 25–50). The Falmer Press.

Deutsch, M. (1985). *Distributive justice. A social-psychological perspective*. Yale University Press.

Dewey, J. (1910). *How we think*. D. C. Heath & Co.

Deyhle, D., Hess, G. A., & LeCompte, M. (1992). Approaching ethical issues for qualitative researchers in education. In M. LeCompte, W. Millroy, & J. Preissle (Eds.), *The handbook of qualitative research in education* (pp. 595–641). Academic Press.

Dreyfus, H., & Dreyfus, S. (1990). What is morality? A phenomenological account of the development of ethical expertise. In D. Rasmussen (Ed.), *Universalism vs. communitarianism. Contemporary debates in ethics* (pp. 237–264). MIT Press.

Driver, J. (2014). The history of utilitarianism. In E. N. Zalta (Ed.), *The Stanford encyclopedia of philosophy* (Winter 2014 ed.). Retrieved May 4, 2021, from https://plato.stanford.edu/archives/win2014/entries/utilitarianism-history/

Durik, A. M., & Harackiewicz, J. M. (2007). Different strokes for different folks: How individual interest moderates the effects of situational factors on task interest. *Journal of Educational Psychology, 99*(3), 597–610.

Dweck, C. S. (2000). *Self-theories. Their role in motivation, personality, and development.* Psychology Press.

Dweck, C. S. (2006). *Mindset. The new psychology of success.* Ballantine Books.

Eisenschmidt, E., Kuusisto, E., Poom-Valickis, K., & Tirri, K. (2019). Virtues that create purpose for ethical leadership: Exemplary principals from Estonia and Finland. *Journal of Beliefs & Values, 40*(4), 433–446.

Fenstermacher, G. D., Osguthorpe, R. D., & Sanger, M. N. (2009). Teaching morally and teaching morality. *Teacher Education Quarterly, 36*, 7–19.

Field, S., Kuczera, M., & Pont, B. (2007). *No more failures: Ten steps to equity in education.* OECD. https://www.oecd.org/education/school/nomorefailurestenstepstoequityineducation.htm

Finlex. (2020). Oppivelvollisuuslaki 1214 [Law of compulsory education 1214]. Retrieved May 5, 2021, from https://www.finlex.fi/fi/laki/ajantasa/2020/20201214

Finnish Parliament. (2020). Lakialoite laiksi rikoslain 21 luvun muuttamisesta [Bill to change criminal law 21]. Retrieved May 4, 2020, from https://www.eduskunta.fi/FI/vaski/PoytakirjaAsiakohta/Sivut/PTK_18+2020+5.aspx

FNBE. (2016). *National core curriculum for basic education 2014.* Finnish National Board of Education.

Forster, D. J. (2019). Codes of professional ethics and conduct in teaching. In M. Peter (Ed.), *Encyclopedia of teacher education.* Springer. https://doi.org/10.1007/978-981-13-1179-6_159-1

Frankena, W. (1963). *Ethics.* Prentice-Hall.

Frankl, V. E. (1988). *Man's search for meaning.* Pocket Books. (Original work published 1946)

Gholami, K., Kuusisto, E., & Tirri, K. (2015). Is ethical sensitivity in teaching culturally bound? Comparing Finnish and Iranian teachers' ethical sensitivity. *Compare: A Journal of Comparative and International Education, 45*(6), 886–907.

Gilligan, C., & Attanucci, J. (1988). Two moral orientations. In C. Gilligan, J. V. Ward, J. McLean Taylor, & B. Bardige (Eds.), *Mapping the moral domain* (pp. 73–86). Harvard University Press.

Haavio, M. (1948). *Opettajapersoonallisuus* [*Teacher personality*]. Gummerus.

Habermas, J. (1984). *The theory of communicative action. 1: Reason and the rationalization of society.* Heinemann.

Hanhimäki, E., & Tirri, K. (2009). Education for ethically sensitive teaching in critical incidents at school. *Journal of Education for Teaching, 35*(2), 107–121.

Hansen, D. T. (1995). *The call to teach.* Teachers College Press.

Harrison, T. (2019). Virtue ethics in teacher education. In M. Peters (Ed.), *Encyclopedia of teacher education*. Springer. https://doi.org/10.1007/978-981-13-1179-6

Hedayati, N. (2019). *Values and morality in Iranian schools* [Doctoral dissertation, University of Helsinki]. Helda. http://urn.fi/URN:ISBN:978-951-51-5637-2

Hedayati, N., Kuusisto, E., Gholami, K., & Tirri, K. (2017a). Gender-specific religious moral dilemmas in Iranian schools. In R. M. Elmesky, C. C. Yeakey, & O. Marcucci (Eds.), *The power of resistance: Culture, ideology and social reproduction in global contexts* (pp. 365–381). Emerald Group Publishing Limited.

Hedayati, N., Kuusisto, E., Gholami, K., & Tirri, K. (2017b). Value learning trajectories in Iranian educational system. In A. Kuusisto & L. Gearon (Eds.), *Value learning trajectories. Theory, method, context* (pp. 179–194). Waxmann.

Hedayati, N., Kuusisto, E., Gholami, K., & Tirri, K. (2017c). Life purposes of Iranian secondary school students. *Journal of Moral Education, 46*(3), 283–294.

Hedayati, N., Kuusisto, E., Gholami, K., & Tirri, K. (2019). Moral conflicts in Iranian secondary schools. *Journal of Beliefs & Values, 40*, 464–476.

Herbart, J. F. (1835). *Umriss pädagogischer Vorlesungen* (H. Wendt, Ed.). Verlag von Philipp Reclam.

Hofstede, G., Hofstede, G. J., & Minkov, M. (2010). *Cultures and organizations. Software of the mind* (3rd ed.). McGraw-Hill. (Original work published 1991)

Hopmann, S. (2007). Restrained teaching: The common core of Didaktik. *European Educational Research Journal, 6*(2), 109–124.

Huberman, M. (1992). *The lives of teachers* (J. Marti, Trans.). Cassell. (Original work published 1989)

Hulleman, C., & Harackiewicz, J. M. (2009). Promoting interest and performance in high school science classes. *Science, 326*(5958), 1410–1412.

Hursthouse, R., & Pettigrove, G. (2018). Virtue ethics. In E. N. Zalta (Ed.), *The Stanford encyclopedia of philosophy* (Winter 2018 ed.). Retrieved May 4, 2021, from https://plato.stanford.edu/archives/win2018/entries/ethics-virtue/

Husu, J., & Tirri, K. (2001). Teachers' ethical choices in sociomoral settings. *Journal of Moral Education, 30*(4), 361–375.

Husu, J., & Tirri, K. (2007). Developing whole school pedagogical values: A case of going through the ethos of 'good schooling.' *Teaching and Teacher Education, 23*(4), 390–401.

Jackson, P., Boostrom, R., & Hansen, D. (1993). *The moral life of schools*. Jossey-Bass Publishers.

Jiang, F., & Gao, D. (2018). Are Chinese preservice teachers' life purposes associated with their perceptions of how much their university supports community service work? *Journal of Moral Education, 47*(2), 201–216.

Kamins, M., & Dweck, C. S. (1999). Person vs. process praise and criticism: Implications for contingent self-worth and coping. *Developmental Psychology, 35*(3), 835–847.

Kansanen, P., & Meri, M. (1999). The didactic relation in the teaching-studying-learning process. In B. Hudson, F. Buchenberger, P. Kansanen, & H. Seel (Eds.), *Didaktik/Fachdidaktik as science(-s) of the teaching profession?* (Vol. 2, No 1, pp. 107–116). TNTEE Publications.

Kansanen, P., Tirri, K., Meri, M., Krokfors, L., Husu, J., & Jyrhämä, R. (2000). *Teachers' pedagogical thinking. Theoretical landscapes, practical challenges.* Peter Lang.

Kant, I. (2007). *Anthropology, history and education* (G. Zöller & R. Louden, Eds., M. Gregor, Trans.). Cambridge University Press. (Original work published 1803)

Kaukko, M., Wilkinson, J., & Kohli, R. K. (2021). Pedagogical love in Finland and Australia: A study of refugee children and their teachers. *Pedagogy, Culture & Society.* https://doi.org/10.1080/14681366.2020.1868555

Kohlberg, L. (1969). Stage and sequence: The cognitive-developmental approach to socialization. In D. A. Goslin (Ed.), *Handbook of socialization theory and research* (pp. 347–480). Rand McNally.

Kujala, T., & Näätänen, R. (2010). The adaptive brain: A neurophysiological perspective. *Progress in Neurobiology, 91*(1), 55–67.

Kuusimäki, A.-M., Uusitalo-Malmivaara, L., & Tirri, K. (2019). Parents' and teachers' views on digital communication in Finland. *Education Research International.* doi:10.1155/2019/8236786

Kuusisto, E., Gholami, K., & Tirri, K. (2016). Finnish and Iranian teachers' views on their competence to teach purpose. *Journal of Education for Teaching, 42*(5), 541–555.

Kuusisto, E., Laine, S., & Tirri, K. (2017). How do school children and adolescents perceive the nature of talent development? A case study from Finland. *Education Research International.* doi:10.1155/2017/4162957

Kuusisto, E., & Tirri, K. (2013). Kasvun ajattelutapa opettajilla ja vanhemmilla: Tapaustutkimus suomalaisista kouluista [Growth mindset of teachers and parents: A case study of Finnish schools]. In *Uusi oppiminen* [*New learning*] (pp. 14–34). Finnish parliament, Committee for the Future.

Kuusisto, E., & Tirri, K. (2019). Teachers' moral competence in pedagogical encounters. In W. Veugelers (Ed.), *Education for democratic intercultural citizenship* (pp. 81–106). Brill Sense.

Kuusisto, E., & Tirri, K. (2021). The challenge of educating purposeful teachers in Finland. *Education Sciences, 11*(1), 29.

Kuusisto, E., Tirri, K., & Rissanen, I. (2012). Finnish teachers' ethical sensitivity. *Education Research International.* doi:10.1155/2012/351879

Kuusisto, E., Ubani, M., Nokelainen, P., & Toom, A. (Eds.). (2021). *Good teachers for tomorrow's schools: Purpose, values and talents in education.* Brill.

Kärkkäinen, R., & Räty, H. (2010). Parents' and teachers' views of the child's academic potential. *Educational Studies, 36*, 229–232.

Laine, S., Kuusisto, E., & Tirri, K. (2016). Finnish teachers' conceptions of giftedness. *Journal for the Education of the Gifted, 39*(2), 151–167.

Laine, S., & Tirri, K. (2016). How Finnish elementary school teachers meet the needs of their gifted students. *High Ability Studies, 27*(2), 149–164.

Lebacqz, K. (1985). *Professional ethics. Power and paradox*. Abingdon Press.

Levinthal, C. (2022). *Parental engagement with children's learning in Finland and Portugal* [Doctoral dissertation, University of Helsinki]. (Under review)

Levinthal, C., Kuusisto, E., & Tirri, K. (2021). Finnish and Portuguese parents' perspectives on the role of teachers in parent-teacher partnerships and parental engagement. *Education Sciences, 11*, 306. https://doi.org/10.3390/educsci11060306

Mäkinen, M. (2013). Becoming engaged in inclusive practices: Narrative reflections on teaching as descriptors of teachers' work engagement. *Teaching and Teacher Education, 35*, 51–61.

Malin, H. (2018). *Teaching for purpose. Preparing students for lives of meaning*. Harvard Education Press.

Malin, H., Reilly, T. S., Quinn, B., & Moran, S. (2013). Adolescent purpose development: Exploring empathy, discovering roles, shifting priorities, and creating pathways. *Journal of Research on Adolescence, 24*(1), 186–199.

Malin, H., Tirri, K., & Liauw, I. (2015). Adolescent moral motivations for civic engagement: Clues to the political gender gap? *Journal of Moral Education, 44*(1), 34–50.

Manninen, N. (2019). *Social services students' education and purposes in life: A case study from Finland* [Doctoral dissertation, University of Helsinki]. Helda. http://urn.fi/URN:ISBN:978-951-51-5167-4

Manninen, N., Kuusisto, E., & Tirri, K. (2018). Life goals of Finnish social services students. *Journal of Moral Education, 47*, 175–185.

Mauranen, A., Aro, E.-M., Hari, R., Jalkanen, S., Kulmala, M., Mustajoki, A., Nieminen, R., Niiniluoto, I., Raivio, K., Sipilä, J., & Tirri, K. (2021). *Bending, but not breaking – From the coronavirus pandemic to strengthening Finland's crisis resilience*. Finnish Academy of Science and Letters.

Maxwell, B., Boon, H., Tanchuk, N., & Rauwerdab, B. (2021). Adaptation and validation of a test of ethical sensitivity in teaching. *Journal of Moral Education, 50*(3), 267–292.

Moran, S. (2009). Purpose: Giftedness in intrapersonal intelligence. *High Ability Studies, 20*(2), 143–159.

Moran, S. (2019). Is personal life purpose replacing shared worldview as youth increasingly individuate? Implications for educators. *International Journal of Learning, Teaching and Educational Research, 18*(5), 8–23.

Narvaez, D. (2001). *Ethical sensitivity. Activity booklet 1*. Retrieved March 2, 2007, from http://www.nd.edu/~dnarvaez/

Narvaez, D., & Endicott, L. G. (2009). *Ethical sensitivity. Nurturing character in the classroom* (Ethex Series Book 1). Alliance for Catholic Education Press.

Nash, R. (2002). *'Real world' ethics. Frameworks for educators and human service professionals* (2nd ed.). Teachers College Press. (Original work published 1996)

Noddings, N. (1984). *Caring. A feminine approach to ethics and moral education.* University of California Press.

Noddings, N. (1992). *The challenge to care in schools.* Teachers College Press.

Nurmi, J.-E. (1991). How do adolescents see their future? A review of the development of future orientation and planning. *Developmental Review, 11*(1), 1–59.

Oser, F. (1986). Moral education and values education: The discourse perspective. In M. Wittrock (Ed.), *Handbook of research on teaching* (pp. 917–941). Macmillan.

Oser, F. (1991). Professional morality: A discourse approach (the case of the teaching profession). In W. Kurtines & J. Gewirtz (Eds.), *Handbook of moral behavior and development. Vol. 2: Research* (pp. 191–228). Lawrence Erlbaum Associates.

Oser, F. (1992). Morality on professional action: A discourse approach for teaching. In F. Oser, A. Dick, & J.-L. Patry (Eds.), *Effective and responsible teaching: The new synthesis* (pp. 109–125). Jossey-Bass.

Oser, F., & Althof, W. (1993). Trust in advance: On the professional morality of teachers. *Journal of Moral Education, 22*(3), 253–275.

Oser, F., & Biedermann, H. (2018). The professional ethos of teachers. Is only a procedural discourse. Approach a suitable model? In A. Weinberger, H. Biedermann, J-L. Patry, & S. Weyringer (Eds.), *Professionals' ethos and education for responsibility* (pp. 23–39). Sense.

Osguthorpe, R. D. (2021). Historical perspective on the moral character of teachers. In F. Oser, K. Heinrichs, J. Bauer, & T. Lovat (Eds.), *The international handbook of teacher ethos: Strengthening teachers, supporting learners* (pp. 9–24). Springer.

Österman, K., Björkqvist, K., & Wahlbeck, K. (2014). Twenty-eight years after the complete ban on the physical punishment of children in Finland: Trends and psychosocial concomitants. *Aggressive Behavior, 40*, 568–581.

Peters, R. (1966). *Ethics and education.* Allen & Unwin.

Piaget, J. (1965). *The moral judgement of the child* (M. Gabain, Trans.). Free Press. (Original work published 1932)

Pyhältö, K., Pietarinen, J., Haverinen, K., Tikkanen, L., & Soini, T. (2021). Teacher burnout profiles and proactive strategies. *European Journal of Psychology of Education, 36*, 219–242.

Rest, J. (1983). Morality. In P. Mussen (Ed.), *Carmichael's manual of child psychology* (4th ed., Vol. 3, pp. 556–629). Wiley.

Rissanen, I., Kuusisto, E., Hanhimäki, E., & Tirri, K. (2018a). Teachers' implicit meaning systems and their implications for pedagogical thinking and practice: A case study from Finland. *Scandinavian Journal of Educational Research, 62*(4), 487–500.

Rissanen, I., Kuusisto, E., Hanhimäki, E., & Tirri, K. (2018b). The implications of teachers' implicit theories for moral education: A case study from Finland. *Journal of Moral Education, 47*(1), 63–77.

Rissanen, I., Kuusisto, E., Tuominen, M., & Tirri, K. (2019). In search of a growth mindset pedagogy: A case study of one teacher's classroom practices in a Finnish elementary school. *Teaching and Teacher Education, 77,* 204–213. https://doi.org/10.1016/j.tate.2018.10.002

Rissanen, I., Laine, S., Puusepp, I., Kuusisto, E., & Tirri, K. (2021). Implementing and evaluating growth mindset pedagogy -A study of Finnish elementary school teachers. *Frontiers in Education.* https://doi.org/10.3389/feduc.2021.753698

Roberts, B. W., & Robins, R. W. (2000). Broad dispositions, broad aspirations: The intersection of personality traits and major life goals. *Personality and Social Psychology Bulletin, 26*(10), 1284–1296.

Rohlf, M. (2020). Immanuel Kant. In E. N. Zalta (Ed.), *The Stanford encyclopedia of philosophy* (Fall 2020 ed.). Retrieved May 4, 2021, from https://plato.stanford.edu/archives/fall2020/entries/kant/

Ronkainen, R., Kuusisto, E., & Tirri, K. (2019). Growth mindset in teaching: A case study of a Finnish elementary school teacher. *International Journal of Learning, Teaching and Educational Research, 18*(8), 141–154.

Ronkainen, R., Kuusisto, E., Eisenschmidt, E., & Tirri, K. (2021). Ethical sensitivity of Finnish and Estonian teachers. *Journal of Moral Education.* https://doi.org/10.1080/03057240.2021.1960491

Ross, W. D. (1930). *The right and the good.* Clarendon Press.

Ryff, C. D. (1989). Happiness is everything, or is it? Explorations on the meaning of psychological well-being. *Journal of Personality and Social Psychology, 57,* 1069–1081.

Ryff, C. D., & Keyes, C. L. M. (1995). The structure of psychological well-being revisited. *Journal of Personality and Social Psychology, 69*(4), 719–727.

Sahlberg, P. (2011). *Finnish lessons. What can the world learn from educational change in Finland?* Teachers College Press.

Salmela-Aro, K., Hietajärvi, L., & Lonka, K. (2019). Work burnout and engagement profiles among teachers. *Frontiers in Psychology, 10,* 2254.

Salmivalli, C. (2010). Bullying and the peer group: A review. *Aggression and violent behavior, 15*(2), 112–120.

Salmivalli, C., Kärnä, A., & Poskiparta, E. (2011). Counteracting bullying in Finland: The KiVa-program and its effects on different forms of being bullied. *International Journal of Behavioral Development, 35*(5), 405–411.

Schön, D. (1983). *The reflective practitioner. How professionals think in action.* Basic Books.

Schwimmer, M., & Maxwell, B. (2017). Codes of ethics and teachers' professional autonomy. *Ethics and Education, 12*(2), 141–152.

Shulman, L. S. (1986). Those who understand: Knowledge growth in teaching. *Educational Researcher, 15*(2), 4–14.

Shulman, L. S. (1987). Knowledge and teaching: Foundations of the new reform. *Harvard Educational Review, 57*(1), 1–23.

Sockett, H. (1993). *The moral base for teacher professionalism.* Teachers College Press.

Stadius, G. (1967). *Synpunkter på Herman Nohls bildningsteori.* Acta Academiae Aboenseis A, Humaniora 34:1. Åbo Akademi.

Steger, M. F., Frazier, P., Oishi, S., & Kaler, M. (2006). The meaning in life questionnaire: Assessing the presence of and search for meaning in life. *Journal of Counseling Psychology, 53*(1), 80–93.

Terhart, E. (1998). Formalised codes of ethics for teachers: Between professional autonomy and administrative control. *European Journal of Education, 33*(4), 433–444.

Tirri, K. (1998). *Koulu moraalisena yhteisönä [School as a moral community].* University of Helsinki.

Tirri, K. (1999a). *Opettajan ammattietiikka [Teacher's professional ethics].* WSOY.

Tirri, K. (1999b). Teachers' perceptions of moral dilemmas at school. *Journal of Moral Education, 28*(1), 31–47.

Tirri, K. (2002). Opetustyön keskeiset eettiset ongelmakohdat [The central ethical challenges in teaching]. In R. Sarras & Opetusalan eettinen neuvottelukunta (Eds.), *Etiikka koulun arjessa [Ethics in everyday school life]* (pp. 150–167). Otava.

Tirri, K. (2003a). The moral concerns and orientations of sixth-and ninth-grade students. *Educational Research and Evaluation, 9*(1), 93–108.

Tirri, K. (2003b). The teacher's integrity. In F. Oser & W. Veugelers (Eds.), *Teaching in moral and democratic education* (pp. 65–81). Peter Lang.

Tirri, K. (Ed.). (2008). *Educating moral sensibilities in urban schools.* Brill.

Tirri, K. (2010). Teachers' values underlying their professional ethics. In T. Lovat, R. Toomey, & N. Clement (Eds.), *International research handbook on values education and student well-being* (pp. 153–163). Springer.

Tirri, K. (2012). The core of school pedagogy: Finnish teachers' views of the educational purposefulness of their teaching. In H. Niemi, A. Toom, & A. Kallioniemi (Eds.), *Miracle of education* (pp. 55–66). Sense Publishers.

Tirri, K. (2014). The last 40 years in Finnish teacher education. *Journal of Education for Teaching, 23*, 1–10.

Tirri, K. (2017). Finland – ethics and equality. In W. Veugelers, I. de Groot, & V. Stolk (Eds.), *Research for CULT Committee – Teaching common values in Europe* (pp. 83–90). European Parliament, Policy Department for Structural and Cohesion Policies.

Tirri, K. (2018). The purposeful teacher. In R. B. Monya (Ed.), *Teacher education in the 21st century* (pp. 221–229). IntechOpen.

Tirri, K., Eisenschmidt, E., Poom-Valickis, K., & Kuusisto, E. (2021). Current challenges in school leadership in Estonia and Finland: A multiple case study among exemplary principals. *Education Research International.* https://doi.org/10.1155/2021/8855927

Tirri, K., & Husu, J. (2002). Care and responsibility in 'the best interest of the child': Relational voices of ethical dilemmas in teaching. *Teachers and Teaching, 8*(1), 65–80.

Tirri, K., & Husu, J. (2006). The pedagogical values behind teachers' reflection of school ethos. In M. B. Klein (Ed.), *New teaching and teacher issues* (pp. 163–182). Nova Science Publishers.

Tirri, K., Husu, J., & Kansanen, P. (1999). The epistemological stance between the knower and the known. *Teaching and Teacher Education, 15*(8), 911–922.

Tirri, K., & Kuusisto, E. (2013). How Finland serves gifted and talented pupils. *Journal for the Education of the Gifted, 36*(1), 84–96.

Tirri, K., & Kuusisto, E. (2016a). Finnish preservice teachers' perceptions on the role of purpose in teaching. *Journal of Education for Teaching, 42*(5), 532–540.

Tirri, K., & Kuusisto, E. (2016b). How can purpose be taught? *Journal of Religious Education, 64*(2), 101–112.

Tirri, K., & Kuusisto, E. (2019). *Opettajan ammattietiikkaa oppimassa [Learning teacher's professional ethics]*. Gaudeamus.

Tirri, K., & Kuusisto, E. (2022). *Inclusive education from the perspective of teachers' professional ethics – The case of Finnish teachers* [Manuscript under review].

Tirri, K., & Laine, S. (2017a). Inclusive education in teacher education. In D. J. Clandinin & J. Husu (Eds.), *The Sage handbook of research on teacher education, Vol. 2* (pp. 761–776). Sage.

Tirri, K., & Laine, S. (2017b). Ethical challenges in inclusive education: The case of gifted students. In A. Gaweski (Ed.), *Ethics, equity, and inclusive education. International perspectives on inclusive education, Vol. 9* (pp. 239–257). Emerald Group Publishing.

Tirri, K., Moran, S., & Mariano, J. M. (2016). Education for purposeful teaching around the world: Introduction. *Journal of Education for Teaching, 42*(5), 526–531.

Tirri, K., & Nokelainen, P. (2007). Comparison of academically average and gifted students' self-rated ethical sensitivity. *Educational Research and Evaluation, 13*(6), 587–601.

Tirri, K., & Nokelainen, P. (2011). *Measuring multiple intelligences and moral sensitivities in education.* Sense Publishers.

Tirri, K., & Pehkonen, L. (2002). The moral reasoning and scientific argumentation of gifted adolescents. *The Journal of Secondary Gifted Education, 13*, 120–129.

Tirri, K., & Puolimatka, T. (2000). Teacher authority in schools: A case study from Finland. *Journal of Education for Teaching, 26*(2), 157–165.

Tirri, K., Toom, A., & Husu, J. (2013). The moral matters of teaching: A Finnish perspective. In C. J. Graig, P. C. Meijer, & J. Broeckmans (Eds.), *From teacher thinking to teachers and teaching. The evolution of a research community* (pp. 223–239). Emerald Group Publishing Limited.

Tirri, K., & Ubani, M. (2013). Education of Finnish preservice teachers for purposeful teaching. *Journal of Education for Teaching, 39*(1), 21–29.

Toom, A. (2006). *Tacit pedagogical knowing. At the core of teacher's professionality.* Yliopistopaino.

Toom, A., Husu, J., & Tirri, K. (2015). Cultivating preservice teachers' moral competencies in teaching during teacher education. In C. Craig & L. Orland-Barak (Eds.), *International teacher education. Promising pedagogies: Vol. 3* (pp. 13–31). Emerald Group Publishing Limited.

Trade Union of Education in Finland. (2010). *Ethical principles of teaching.* Retrieved January 5, 2021, from https://www.oaj.fi/en/education/ethical-principles-of-teaching/teachers-values-and-ethical-principles/

Trade Union of Education in Finland. (2017). *Comenius oath.* Retrieved January 5, 2021, from https://www.oaj.fi/en/education/ethical-principles-of-teaching/comenius-oath-for-teachers/

UNESCO. (2021). *Reimagining our futures together. A new social contract for education.* Report from the international commission on the futures of education. https://unesdoc.unesco.org/ark:/48223/pf0000379707.locale=en

Usher, E. L., & Pajares, F. (2008). Sources of self-efficacy in school: Critical review of the literature and future directions. *Review of Educational Research, 78*(4), 751–796.

Veugelers, W. (2017). The moral in Paulo Freire's educational work: What moral education can learn from Paulo Freire. *Journal of Moral Education, 46,* 412–421.

Veugelers, W., de Groot, I., & Stolk, V. (2017). *Research for CULT Committee – Teaching common values in Europe.* European Parliament, Policy Department for Structural and Cohesion Policies.

Vierimaa, K. (2012). *Koulukiusaamisen kriminalisointi [Criminalization of bullying at school]* [Master's thesis, University of Lapland]. Lauda. http://urn.fi/URN:NBN:fi:ula-201203011034

Wikipedia. 2021. *Kuritus* [Discipline]. Retrieved May 4, 2021, from https://fi.wikipedia.org/wiki/Kuritus

Yeager, D. S., Trzesniewski, K. H., Tirri, K., Nokelainen, P., & Dweck, C. S. (2011). Adolescents' implicit theories predict desire for vengeance after remembered and hypothetical peer conflicts: Correlational and experimental evidence. *Developmental Psychology, 47*(4), 1090–1107.

Zhang, J. (2020). *Mindset in learning: A cross-cultural study in China and Finland* [Doctoral dissertation, University of Helsinki]. Helda. http://urn.fi/URN:ISBN:978-951-51-6759-0

Zhang, J., Kuusisto, E., & Tirri, K. (2020a). Same mindset, different pedagogical strategies: A case study comparing Chinese and Finnish teachers. *International Journal of Learning, Teaching and Educational Research, 19*(2), 248–263.

Zhang, J., Kuusisto, E., Nokelainen, P., & Tirri, K. (2020b). Peer feedback reflects the mindset and academic motivation of learners. *Frontiers in Psychology, 11*(1701).

Index

Printed in the United States
by Baker & Taylor Publisher Services